# Making
# Markets

# Making Markets

*How Firms Can Design
and Profit from Online Auctions
and Exchanges*

## Ajit Kambil
## Eric van Heck

HARVARD BUSINESS SCHOOL PRESS
BOSTON, MASSACHUSETTS

Requests for permission to use or reproduce material from this book
should be directed to permissions@hbsp.harvard.edu, or mailed to
Permissions, Harvard Business School Publishing, 60 Harvard Way,
Boston, Massachusetts 02163.

**Library of Congress Cataloging-in-Publication Data**

Kambil, Ajit, 1962–
    Making markets : how firms can design and profit from online
auctions and exchanges / Ajit Kambil, Eric van Heck.
        p. cm.
Includes bibliographical references and index.
    ISBN 1-57851-658-7 (alk. paper)
  1.  Internet marketing. 2.  Internet auctions. 3.  Industrial marketing.
4.  Marketing—Computer programs. 5.  Electronic commerce.
I. Heck, E. van. II. Title.
    HF5415.1265 .K358 2002
    658.8′4—dc21

                                                        2002000419

# Contents

# Preface

This book began on a cold and wet Dutch morning in the spring of 1992, when Eric took me to the Bloemenveiling Aalsmeer—at that time the largest of the Dutch flower auctions. As we watched, thousands of flower-stacking carts progressed through the auction halls, and hundreds of bidders responded to multiple pricing clocks as they sipped their steaming cups of morning coffee. We became fascinated by the institutional realities of markets and auctions.

It was then that we got a partial answer to my irreverent question: Why are the Dutch any good at flowers? After all, they have expensive land, expensive labor, and not the best of weather. As we walked through the flower market, itself as big as a hundred soccer fields, and learned more about the pricing, logistics, and distribution requirements of this fragile product, we began to discover how the Dutch retained their competitive edge in this industry. We saw how they brought these flowers in from all over the world, priced them, packaged them into new assortments, and then shipped them out again—sometimes back to the same country of origin. We also came to realize how fragile these markets themselves were, and how information technology could potentially undermine them, by decoupling the informational trading processes from the logistics processes.

As we learned more about electronic market initiatives and failures in the Dutch flower industry, we decided to follow the story of these auctions as institutions and expand our studies. Over the years Eric had specialized in the study of electronic auctions, while I had undertaken a broader portfolio of research in electronic commerce, markets, venturing, and strategy. Both of us had wanted to know how one could more effectively design and implement markets. This book represents a pause in our learning, as we frame our shared understanding into words.

But this book is more than a mere reflection. We believe that managers today stand at the edge of a chasm separating early adopters and mainstream users. They need to choose between making electronic markets a critical strategic tool for their organizations or not adopting them at all, based on watching many B2B electronic market initiatives flame out. Our objective in this book is to help managers cross that chasm by providing information that managers can use to design, create, and participate in electronic markets. We believe that electronic markets will continue to grow in importance and have increasingly diverse and strategic business applications. Some of the strategic applications we discuss in this book are still in their infancy, but we believe they will become part of common business practices by the end of the decade.

The dramatic advances in information technology continue to provide a strong foundation for market applications in most spheres of business. What lags behind is the knowledge of how to create and effectively use markets—the social consensus, the understanding, and the will to apply electronic markets to many business contexts. Indeed, as we wrote this book, we realized that our audience would not consist of "chief electronic markets officers"—that job title doesn't exist yet.

In the course of the next decade, however, electronic markets and auctions will become an important tool to many managers, from the chief marketing officers and the managers responsible for supply chains, operations, and logistics to the CEOs themselves. Since this book covers a wide range of market applications—business-to-customer, business-to-business, and interenterprise applications—it should help a variety of high-level executives better understand and formulate strategies for making and using markets.

This book is also a step toward closing the knowledge gap on effective market design. For us, markets are not simple economics-textbook abstractions. While we acknowledge the extensive research findings about auctions and market design as well as the contributions of economists, we find much of this material cloaked in the formalisms of game theory and generally inaccessible to practicing managers. This book is not about game theory, nor is it narrowly focused on designing specific auction mechanisms. Instead, we focus on the pragmatic and emerging applications of markets and the factors that lead to their successful deployment in creating business value.

This book builds on our own study of markets over the last decade. During this time we have:

- Followed nearly one hundred case studies of electronic markets, some through interviews with senior executives who have created or used electronic markets, some through our own observations of the market, and others through the analysis of secondary sources (Web sites, press reports, key informants). We have followed some of the cases—like the Dutch flower auctions—in detail for a decade.

- Surveyed market makers in the United States and Europe, analyzing their successes and failures. We undertook a survey of different pricing mechanisms in the United States and a survey of Web auctions in Europe. Several in-depth studies were undertaken to analyze eBay and Yahoo! auctions.

- Completed select laboratory experiments related to multi-attribute auctions, auction speed, and the winner's curse.

- Designed new market systems such as knowledge exchanges.

- Advised clients on designing, building, and implementing electronic markets.

Although we've focused this book on the design of online or electronic markets, we have not done so exclusively. We think useful lessons can also be learned from traditional physical markets. Therefore, the cases and stories we have chosen deal with all three: traditional "brick and mortar" markets, combinations of electronic and traditional markets, and purely electronic markets.

We hope this book will stimulate managers to use electronic markets more effectively and appropriately in a range of organizational and industry applications. We also hope it stimulates business schools to reframe their curricula and build interdisciplinary classes that teach students the design of markets. Business schools have spent a lot of time teaching students about organizational behavior and design, but hardly any time in the study of market institutions—a critical infrastructure for commerce in the past and in the new century that we live in today.

# Acknowledgments

In the writing of this book, we have benefited enormously from the ideas and experiences of many knowledgeable people.

We would like to thank our colleagues: Jeff Brooks, Susan Cantrell, and Paul Nunes at the Accenture Institute for Strategic Change helped shape key ideas around a portfolio approach to market participation, resale markets, and all-in-one markets. With the support of Mike May and under the leadership of Tom Davenport, the Institute has set the standard for successful management research and publication of thought leadership. We have also benefited tremendously from Accenture's Supply Chain Service Line. Bill Copacino, Ed Starr, Roger Dik, Donavon Favre, M. Scott Sparks, Jonathan Whitaker, Jay Holata, and Jay Stephens all contributed enormously to our understanding of B2B markets, their governance, and their evolution.

This book also builds on a stream of research started more than a decade ago at MIT. Marvin Sirbu, now at Carnegie-Mellon, first introduced Ajit to the theory of the firm and transaction-cost economics as the post-divestiture structure of the telecommunications industry was examined. Tom Malone (who supervised Ajit's master's thesis on the effects of IT on vertical integration), Jack Rockart, John Henderson, N. Venkatraman, and Benn Konsynski (who supervised Ajit's Ph.D. thesis on designing technology-mediated exchange relations and networks) have all substantially influenced the development of his ideas on markets.

At the Rotterdam School of Management, Otto Koppius provided useful feedback on an earlier version of the manuscript, and Ben Leijdekkers, Jochem Paarlberg, Jimmy Tseng, Peter Vervest, and Matthijs Wolters helped to gather data, set up experiments, and refine ideas on different aspects of electronic markets and auctions. Accenture and the Erasmus Research Institute of Management provided grants to conduct research and work on this book. Experimental research with electronic auctions was carried out in the Eneco Trading Room, and Neximus provided a software tool to develop electronic auction software.

The enthusiastic leadership of Jo van Nunen as head of the department and Paul Verhaegen as dean of the faculty provided the right stimulus. Dré Kampfraath and Peter Zuurbier at Wageningen University supervised Eric's Ph.D. thesis on design management of electronic data interchange systems and introduced him a long time ago to the Dutch flower industry, which became the starting point of this journey.

This manuscript would not have been complete or readable within a year without the encouragement of our HBS Press senior editor, Melinda Adams Merino, and the magic of Erik Calonius, who helped us convert our dry prose into more engaging text. In the final stages of development, Anne Quaadgras was critical in undertaking the research and managing the drafts through to completion. We are also grateful to the anonymous reviewers who read the earlier versions of the manuscript and provided very useful feedback.

In closing, we would also like to thank our spouses and children for their patience and great support over the course of the last two years. Anne, Tina, and Rita, and Lia, Julia, Simon, and Maartje—thank you!

*Ajit Kambil, Arlington, Massachusetts*
*Eric van Heck, Rotterdam*

# Making
# Markets

# 1

## Seizing the Value of Markets

PARTMINER, A GLOBAL SUPPLIER of electronic components, was not alone when it started its first online market in June 2000. At least 100 other electronic markets had already rushed onto the Internet, and more were on their way.

The initial boom, of course, was short lived. In the end, dozens of the electronic markets went down in flames. In the B2B market alone, their names included Surplus-Bin (auto parts and electronics), Chemdex (life sciences), Promedix (medical products), RedLadder.com (construction), IndustrialVortex (industrial products), BizBuyer (office supplies), and Pradium (agricultural commodities), among many others.

But PartMiner survived. It survived not because it had found a unique market or a particularly new technology. It survived because it had found a successful *strategy*.

PartMiner's initial strategy was to give customers free access to the CAPS Xpert database—the electronics industry's most comprehensive listing of components and related information. Never mind that PartMiner had spent $100 million to acquire the database. The idea was to attract visitors to the Web site.

But that's not all. In its "FreeTradeZone," PartMiner also gave customers four valuable services: the "Research Center," which provided information on more than 15 million parts;

1

"PartMiner Find," which allowed buyers to get quotes for components from twenty major vendors; "PartMiner Buy and Sell," which provided an electronic request for quote, pricing, and purchase order service; and "PartMinerQuote," which generated quotes for hard-to-find electronics components. PartMiner provided all the services for free. So how did they make their money?

The answer is that the company made most of its money from its PartMiner Direct Shopping service. In this service, PartMiner helped buyers (about 2 percent of them) locate parts that they could not find in the free directories. To do so, PartMiner had product buyers who would scour the world markets until they found what was required.

In return, PartMiner made as much as a 30 percent markup on the goods. The company also made money by reselling its database and other services to companies like Dell and Celestica. From 1999 to 2000, revenues almost doubled, from $76 million to $134 million.[1]

PartMiner exemplifies the core message of this book: It is not enough to find a new market for online commerce, or even to be the "first mover" there. What counts is a strategy, one that lays out how you will design the markets, how you will implement them, and ultimately how you will seize value and make money through them.

It's not easy. In the last few years, we've learned a lot of bitter lessons about electronic markets. We've learned that some things don't trade as easily in cyberspace as they do in the physical world. We've learned that some human relationships—which are critical to trading—are not as easy to replicate in cyberspace as others. We've learned that some electronic markets ought to be run in-house by the company, but that others should be outsourced. And we've learned that some electronic markets shouldn't be started at all.

To play this game in cyberspace, companies must recognize the rules that govern electronic markets. That's what this book is all about. In it, we will show you where best to use electronic markets, how to design them, and how to implement them. We will show you how firms that master these challenges will achieve competitive advantage, while others will fail.

## Key Insights

Several insights will resonate time and again throughout this book. Many of these were not considered at all in the first years of electronic markets. Others were considered but never given enough weight to make a significant difference in strategy and operations. Now, with history as our guide, they provide lessons that should not be forgotten again.

The first is that electronic markets are *not* technological interactions supported by humans. They are human interactions supported by technology. This is a critical distinction and certainly the one that caused electronic markets in the 1990s to fail more than any other reason. As you will read in subsequent pages, human beings have always made markets, and they will continue to do so in the future—even if business is conducted through cyberspace. With that thought in mind, you must always incorporate the effects of human behavior in markets, in terms of both the design and use of the markets. You must also create a social context for trading, one that is similar to traditional markets. And you must think very hard before replacing the middleman in electronic markets—in many cases, disintermediation through technology does not work.

Second, cyberspace markets cannot be thin replicas of the traditional market. Rather, they must be as rich, complex, and complete as the traditional markets themselves. Moving a market from place to space in these terms is not easy. You must consider the *basic trade processes*—search, pricing, logistics, payment and settlement, and authentication. You must also consider the *trade context processes*—such things as product representation, regulation, risk management, influence, and dispute resolution. As we explain in the chapters ahead, the devil is in the details.

Third, for an electronic market to succeed, it must create value for *all* the participants. For instance, it must increase access, lower prices, and lower transaction costs. But beyond that, it must prove itself *even better* than what now exists. Electronic markets have many opportunities to do this. Another challenge is that electronic markets must achieve critical mass, fast. If you build it, the customers will come— but only if other customers and suppliers are there first.

Fourth, market makers must be sure that the electronic market they create fits into their existing business processes. This means that existing systems and processes must often be changed to synch up with the electronic market. For example, will the resale market you create conflict with your current sales channels?

Fifth, it's the creative application of electronic markets that will mark the future winners. Electronic markets will not be restricted to physical goods but will also exist for intangibles such as risk management and internal resource allocation. In order to succeed, market makers must create the rules, the processes, and the infrastructure. They will determine the shape of the market—whether it will be a hosted market, an all-in-one market, or a decentralized market, for instance. And they will search for ways to continuously build more value into the market and, over time, for their customers and for themselves.

## The Winning Rules

Several flourishing electronic market companies have learned these new insights and are finding great success in what had been uncharted territories. It's not easy to create and seize the value of markets, but this challenge in itself makes these new markets a compelling potential source for competitive advantage. Because few firms will get it right, the losers will leave the pie to those who do. Among the pioneers are Tele Flower Auction, eBay, and ChemConnect.

## Tele Flower Auction

Tele Flower Auction (TFA) is an electronic market for trading flowers.[2] It was a radical innovation in the Dutch flower industry. Traditionally, flowers were bought and sold in the auction halls of the Dutch flower markets, where buyers would walk by the carts and see the actual flowers up close before bidding. They could search for the exact varieties and growers that interested them, and they could authenticate the quality of the flowers simply by looking at them.

In 1994 the Dutch growers, who own the flower auction houses, implemented restrictions on imported flowers, because they felt threatened by increasing foreign imports of flowers and their negative effect on prices. In response, the East African Flowers group created the Tele Flower Auction. In March 1995, it launched TFA with two growers and seventy buyers.

The TFA allows buyers to bid, Dutch auction style, through personal computer. Before the auctions start, the buyers can search a database of offers and analyze what will be auctioned. The database provides information on the flower lots (producer, product, unit of currency, quality, and minimum purchase quantity) and a digital picture of the flowers. Logistics and price discovery are uncoupled and decentralized: The flowers are not visible to the buyers, and the buyers are not physically present in the auction room. Buyers can earmark lots that interest them, and the software will alert them when those lots are about to be auctioned. The price starts high and drops steadily until a buyer interrupts the process by stopping the clock—signaling acceptance of the price—through his keyboard. The buyer then specifies the quantity he or she wishes to buy, the clock is reset, and the process restarts, continuing until the remainder of the lot is sold. (See chapter 4 for details on the mechanics of a Dutch auction.) Growers send the flowers to the East African Flowers group, which organizes all transport from Nairobi to Holland as well as distribution, payment, and settlement.

TFA succeeded where prior attempts at electronic flower markets had failed. It created compelling value for buyers by permitting renewed access to East African flowers in a more convenient way. It built buyer confidence by establishing stringent quality controls, overseen by the TFA's quality inspectors at the grower's location, at the distribution nexus in Nairobi, and at the TFA center in Holland. In fact, it grew quickly to become the fourth largest flower auction in Holland, and was so successful that other foreign growers wanted to join. TFA permitted them to do so and by 1996 had grown to 35 growers and 160 buyers. However, due to quality and delivery problems with flowers sourced outside of East Africa, TFA refocused its strategy to serve its core customers: East African growers. This has enabled them to grow even more—by 2001 TFA traded flowers from 60 mostly African growers and 125 buyers.

## eBay

Another company that understands the new rules, and is among the innovators in determining the even *newer* rules, is a familiar name to anyone in e-commerce: eBay. Founded in 1995, eBay has evolved from a simple online mechanism to trade collectibles to a place where, in 2001, people bought and sold about $9 billion worth of goods—three times the total sales of Amazon.com. Everything is for sale on eBay—automobiles, jewelry, musical instruments, photographic equipment, computers, furniture, sporting goods, and more. Even the Minnesota house that Bob Dylan grew up in went up for bid on eBay—and sold for $94,600.

How has eBay become the undisputed leader? There are many keys to its success. First, it was able to create a community of users by providing compelling value to buyers and sellers of collectibles by helping them find each other. Its ratings systems and infrastructure for payment and settlement helped to create the trust necessary to trade remotely without having to meet in a flea bazaar. Reputations established on eBay are not easily transferable to other auction sites, creating a lock-in effect with its customers.

But eBay also built the first truly scalable e-commerce model, leveraging its customers to co-create value. eBay holds no inventory and does not have to handle shipping or decide how it will represent the product and advertise it. Customers do it all, saving eBay the costs of fulfillment, warehousing, and a number of other overhead costs. Thus eBay can scale up with minimum investment in physical plant and equipment.

That's not all, though. The company has also killed the competition through smart alliances. The purchase of Butterfields, a traditional auction house, expanded eBay's auction and appraisal expertise. The purchase of Alando and iBazar expanded European operations, and the purchase of Half.com (a site that lists new or used goods for a fixed price) and Billpoint provided eBay with new ways to transact sales and settle payments.

Furthermore, innovations continually change the face of eBay. The site recently added its popular "Buy It Now" feature, for instance, which allows users to grab the item immediately, bypassing the lengthy auction process. eBay has also set up a program that allows businesses to set up "storefronts" on the site. This idea has attracted 18,000 businesses without any promotion, making it one of the largest malls on the Internet. "Buy It Now" and Half.com accounted for 11 percent of eBay revenues and international operations for 14 percent in August 2001.[3]

Through a slew of clever acquisitions and innovations, eBay has managed to grow and prosper. It is a marketplace that could never have existed without the invention of computers and cyberspace. Yet it has retained a human touch that attracts customers by the millions. Everyone benefits from eBay, making its value proposition unassailable. For those who claim that electronic markets don't work, look no farther than the great—and growing—success of eBay.

## ChemConnect

ChemConnect, a seller of chemicals and plastics, is a third company that has learned how to turn electronic markets to its advantage. Its story begins in 1995, when John Beasley proposed the World Chemical Exchange, a place on the Web where buyers and sellers could trade chemical and plastics products.[4] Among the investors that eventually poured more than $100 million into the idea were Accenture, Citigroup, Highland Capital Partners, Morgan Stanley Dean Witter, and SAP Ventures.

The idea itself was a good one, and in November 1999 Dow Chemical chose ChemConnect as a preferred Internet exchange. The site, Dow explained, would not only help them make spot purchases of raw materials, but would also connect them with sellers and buyers from around the world, in real time and in an open and neutral marketplace.[5]

Unwilling to rest on its laurels, ChemConnect continued to innovate online. A most important challenge was to simulate a physical market. With that in mind, it came up with three new ideas. First, it created online "corporate trading rooms." In these "rooms," traders could not only participate in private forward and reverse online auctions, they could also privately negotiate annual contracts and spot transactions.

Second, it developed an "exchange floor," an open, neutral marketplace in cyberspace where buyers and sellers could put up hundreds of postings a day. Third, it created an online "commodities floor," where prequalified members could trade standard, high-volume commodity products in real time. On the floor, their traders could find special trading pits for benzene, propylene, ethylene, naphtha, toluene, and other chemicals. The floor was also connected to trading hubs on the Gulf Coast of the United States, in the Antwerp/Rotterdam region of Europe, and in Singapore.

The company also wanted to give traders a simple way to track their activities, from the purchase orders to the financial settlement and the delivery. To add that value, ChemConnect agreed to merge with Envera, a company that offered supply chain, collaboration, and connectivity tools.

ChemConnect illustrates how successful online markets must stay at the cutting edge of innovation. ChemConnect evolved in less than five years from a message board to an advanced online marketplace, one that supported multiple transaction mechanisms. And while many other B2B markets were dying, in July 2001, ChemConnect was announcing annualized transaction volumes of $3.2 billion—an increase of more than 30 percent over the previous quarter. It said it expected to be profitable within eighteen months, without requiring more cash investment.

*Smart Plays*

Each of the above companies has learned to win mostly by invoking a winning strategy. TFA provided an effective way for its growers to participate in the Dutch flower industry and included all necessary support services under the umbrella of the East African Flowers group. Its strict quality

controls and efficient distribution of flowers from its ware-
houses enabled buyers to purchase flowers without seeing
them in person.

eBay provided a simple mechanism to match buyers and
sellers and introduced reputation rules and payment and settlement methods that created sufficient trust for online
consumer-to-consumer transactions. It then quickly expanded its user base, benefiting from increasing returns to
scale. The greater the number of registered users buying and
putting up things for sale, the more valuable the eBay network became for new participants.

ChemConnect created a neutral and public marketplace,
initially offering only one transaction mechanism to match
suppliers and buyers. But like eBay, it rapidly introduced new
market mechanisms to meet the varied needs of buyers and
sellers. Both eBay and ChemConnect understand that monolithic markets providing a one-size-fits-all solution to trading
no longer satisfy customers. Instead, market makers must
provide multiple transaction mechanisms.

PartMiner mastered the rules of when to automate versus
when to use people to broker transactions. It moved its primary source of value from the brokerage of parts and the pro-
vision of a transaction platform to locating difficult-to-find
parts. By providing the basic electronic market functionality
for free, PartMiner now attracts key customers for its high-
margin sourcing services. Similarly, ChemConnect's merger
with Envera migrates value to end-to-end supply chain management from spot market transactions.

PartMiner and ChemConnect are both adapting to the realities of electronic markets: Simply matching reputable buyers with sellers is very valuable where buyers and sellers may
have had no prior transaction histories. In business markets,
however, buyers and sellers often have long-standing business relationships. The value added by simply matching buy-

ers and sellers is increasingly less than that added in other parts of the transaction, such as coordinating logistics, tracking order fulfillment, and payment and settlement.

## Goals of This Book

The preceding cases illustrate some of the new market rules. In this book we will offer practical rules you can follow to make and seize the value of markets. These rules are derived from our extensive experience in analyzing and designing markets as well as studying various electronic market successes and failures. We think that new electronic market applications will continue to expand the use of online markets. But managers must overcome a number of challenges to capture the value of markets. Although the term "free markets" is widely used to characterize competition, real markets rarely come for free—they must be carefully designed and implemented. The principles we outline in this book will help you design and use markets more successfully.

The next seven chapters address the key issues managers must master to successfully make and use electronic markets. Chapter themes are summarized in the following sections.

### Chapter 2: From Place to Space

Information technologies are transforming key market processes and the very architecture of markets. In this foundational chapter, we introduce the key market processes through which markets create value for buyers and sellers. These include processes related directly to trading—search, pricing, logistics, payment and settlement, and authentication—as well as the trade context processes that can make or break a market—product representation, regulation, risk management, influence, and dispute resolution. We examine the challenges inherent in transitioning these processes from place to space. In the past, these processes were often bound together in one location—an agora, a trade fair, or a stock exchange where people typically met face-to-face. Today they are increasingly physically dispersed, bound together only by communications technology, computing processes, and infrastructures that enable remote trading. Technology creates new architectures for markets, but it also disrupts the status quo. The transition from place to cyberspace is not easy.

Moreover, we are still searching for the right balance between technology and human interaction. As we have learned, technological capabilities change direct trade processes quickly and relatively easily. But it is much harder for technology to move trade context processes—those that require consensus among a community of market participants. Not all market processes can be fully and effectively automated, for instance. We have learned that human beings continue to be at the core of trading and continue to add substantial value to the exchange processes.

### *Chapter 3: Making Markets Work*

In order to switch people from their old ways of trading, new market initiatives must create new value. The value may be in cost savings; speed; better access to products, buyers, and sellers; or even just in adding fun to the process. Markets, after all, are meeting places for communities of buyers, sellers, and market makers. Creating new market alternatives is about recreating the community. If the new market favors only a few, but not all, of the prior participants, it's likely to fail. If market makers want people to come to what they've built, they must be sure that the benefits of the market are great enough to get them there.

We have found that successful market makers not only create a win-win-win situation for all their participants, but they also reduce the risks for the participants as they transition from their previous markets and begin to integrate the new market into their businesses.

We have also found that to succeed, electronic markets must achieve quick critical mass and liquidity. Electronic markets and auctions, after all, become more valuable as more and more traders participate. On the other hand, if critical mass is not achieved quickly, the early adopters (who expected to benefit from the addition of participants) are likely to abandon the market, causing the new market to fail.

Finally, our framework for action provides the blueprint for creating a successful market. To help executives and managers design a logically consistent, high-value marketplace, it asks key questions for each market process. It then helps them look at the strategies and tactics for quickly achieving liquidity.

## *Chapter 4: Auctions: The Devil Is in the Details*

Marketplaces are something like the old Shakespearean plays, in which the audience and the actors interact. In markets the market maker, who is producing the play, must decide on the objectives. How should they be paid? Should they receive fees per transaction, commissions on the value of transactions, subscription charges—or a combination of all three? Is the market maker working to maximize revenues for sellers, cost savings for buyers, or the number of transactions? Depending on the answers, the market maker must design and produce the play—select the market mechanisms, locate the venue for transactions, and operate the market.

To continue the comparison, the genre of the play is determined by the auction methods used in the markets. In this chapter, we will discuss several auction types in terms of their similarities and differences in both processes and outcomes. We look at the trade-offs among auctions and discuss how the improved information access and information-processing capabilities enabled by the Internet allow new types of auctions. These include reverse (buyer-driven) auctions, multi-attribute auctions, and combinatorial auctions.

Next, we will consider how other details can influence price and buying and selling outcomes. Some factors we consider include the number of bidders permitted in the market, the principles for releasing inventory, the methods of representing products, and the kinds of feedback offered bidders. The scripts are still to be written, but market makers and users who master the details of market design will have an edge over those who do not.

## Chapter 5: Using B2B Markets in the Supply Chain

In 1997 and 1998 many companies created new electronic markets. By 2001, many of those had died, and others had changed almost beyond recognition. This chapter examines the changing role of electronic markets in the supply chain, and it answers three questions: How can companies use markets and auctions to realize value in the supply chain? What are the different types of B2B markets? What are the integration challenges companies must overcome?

Reverse auctions provide a compelling example of value creation for supply chain sourcing. In this chapter we review the strategies and tactics companies should consider to exploit the potential of these auctions. More generally, we examine the circumstances that maximize the value of the three major types of B2B markets: independent exchanges, consortia, and private exchanges, as well as the pressures that lead participants to move from one to another.

Electronic markets face many challenges, including the need to manage myriad integration points and, sometimes, the need for a portfolio of market solutions to many problems. But the human factors are among the most interesting, running the gamut from problems arising from the disruption of traditional relationships to the changing of roles and work processes and the need for new skills. How companies manage these issues greatly influences their chances of success. This chapter provides guidance for and examples of successful integration practices.

## Chapter 6: Using Markets Creatively

In this chapter we consider several strategic applications of markets other than supply chains. One of these is resale markets, which allow companies to reach new, value-conscious customer segments while disposing of old goods. These can be a double-edged sword, however. Just as resale markets help companies unload their unwanted inventories, they can also depress the prices of new products if the public determines that it would rather buy used products at auction. As the U.S. economy softened, for instance, Cisco, Nortel, and other companies saw their sales of new products drop, while the resale of their products (pumped onto the market by failing start-ups) boomed. It's no wonder these firms had to take huge write-offs on inventory.

But beyond the tangible goods, markets and auctions are also valuable for intangibles. For example, the use of markets to trade risk and knowledge, to generate predictions of future performance, and to aid in decision making are all beginning to happen. Markets, especially auctions, are a powerful social information-processing mechanism—useful for the social construction of value.

In the past it was difficult to create markets within an organization. This is no longer the case. In the future, markets and auctions will be used as much to connect groups within a firm as to link outsiders. Decision makers will use markets within the firm to trade resources, such as a person's time and knowledge or the use of production facilities and other assets. In a knowledge economy with an overabundance of information, artificial markets may be one of the most powerful mechanisms by which managers can focus their attention on the right information and decide how to allocate key resources in a timely and effective way.

## Chapter 7: Market Tactics

Whether you like it or not, you will increasingly be called upon to participate in electronic markets and auctions. You might need to bid for a contract in a reverse auction or to purchase something through competitive bidding. To do well and avoid the pitfalls of paying too much, you must master the principles of information leverage and understand the psychology of bidding. Markets and auctions can generate tremendous amounts of information about a customer's willingness to pay. As a seller, you can use that information to set your prices more effectively. But it helps bidders, too, for through the market they can determine the extent of the competition and its likely strategies.

Strategically, it is also important to know how much you value something before you enter the bidding. For companies bidding on contracts, this means knowing the value of the customer and the true costs of servicing them. After all, you must avoid bidding too much just to win, a weakness known as the winner's curse. This chapter outlines some principles for participating in markets effectively.

## Chapter 8: Dynamic Market Strategies

Now that you have decided you want to create a market, you must ask yourself a multitude of questions. How do you continue to boost value? Who, if anyone, should own the market with you? How do you build a market strategy into your company? And how do you actually implement the market in your organization, especially when market making is not your core business?

This chapter puts it all together. Market-maker strategies range from differentiation to providing multiple market mechanisms (because one size does *not* fit all). They include creating partnerships and alliances, expanding through mergers and acquisitions, and leveraging market competencies across industries.

Governance issues—who should own the market—are subtle but key to market success. The simple rule to remember is that *market participants will choose the ownership structure that maximizes their benefits and profit potential*. However, its implications are profound.

Market strategy building incorporates three key steps: creating a vision of the electronic market (including the framework for action of chapter 3), selecting the right strategies for market implementation and participation, and finally, mobilizing to implement the market—putting together the nuts and bolts of the marketplace.

## Markets in Context: The Broader Perspective

Markets are just one way to organize trading and resource allocation between a company and its customers, suppliers, employees, and other stakeholders. In the continuum from markets to hierarchies (in which everything is done internally), other ways to organize trading include long-term alliances, joint ventures, long-term employment contracts, standard contracts, and the internalization of key supplier activities within the hierarchy of the firm through direct ownership.

Traditionally, companies typically use internal production capabilities to acquire critical goods or, at the least, commit to long-term contracts with suppliers to get them. But why hasn't the option of sourcing though auctions and outside markets been used more frequently?

Ronald Coase, the Nobel Prize–winning economist, provided the first clear explanation. He recognized that the costs of searching for and writing contingent contracts for trades with external providers were high, and it was often cheaper to internalize these activities through a firm organized as a hierarchy.[6]

Oliver Williamson, the University of California, Berkeley, economist, further developed these ideas to frame and popularize transaction cost economics as driving the choice among markets, hierarchies, and other forms of organization. In trading, transaction costs are those costs buyers or sellers confront to search, negotiate, monitor, safeguard, and resolve trading contracts and agreements. The central idea of transaction cost economics is that firms will choose to acquire and trade resources in a way that reduces both their production and transaction costs.[7]

To be sure, using markets incurs high transaction costs. But outside suppliers may specialize and produce a widget required by multiple buyers, achieving greater economies of scale and production cost advantages over in-house production of the same widget. (Internalizing production is ideal when the widget is very complex and not easy to specify to an outside supplier or in a detailed contract. Thus, the more complex the product, the higher the transaction costs.)

Flexible long-term relationships without detailed contracts, such as with internal employees or key suppliers, can reduce the transaction costs when changes and customization are required. But the production costs may be higher in a firm or in relationships lacking the requisite economies of scale in production.

With electronic communications, especially the Internet, the costs of searching for trading partners, verifying their capabilities, and monitoring contracts fall dramatically. This drastically reduces transaction costs, leading to increased use of markets and outsourcing.[8] The examples in this book illustrate this ongoing transition. Electronic markets change the dynamic, so that going outside for things is a better deal than ever before. Now markets and outside auctions can be truly competitive with either traditional long-term sourcing contracts or internal production.

# 2

## From Place to Space

FOR HUNDREDS OF YEARS, fishermen at the Belgian port of Zeebrugge have hauled in a steady bounty of mussels, clams, herring, eel, and mackerel from the North Sea. And for nearly as long, the port has rung with the shouts of fish traders auctioning the catch to brokers in the early morning light. But on September 14, 1998, centuries of tradition were abruptly broken. The change was initiated by Marie Becaus-Pieters, at the time the managing director of the Zeebrugge fish auction, and soon to become the CEO and "founding mother" of the Pan European Fish Auctions—the first European "virtual" B2B marketplace in the fishing industry.

Becaus-Pieters arrived at the idea of a new marketplace in 1997. She had already watched communications technology transform the Dutch flower industry. Now she realized that the fish markets in her country needed to change as well. It was not that the traditional fish markets were unsuccessful, but that they had not changed since medieval times. In particular, they did not allow fishermen in the North Sea, where supply was abundant, to market their fish easily to the south of Europe, where demand was high. The Internet, Becaus-Pieters realized, was the opportunity to correct the imbalance, selling more fish and at higher prices in the most lucrative markets.

Today, the Pan European Fish Auctions (PEFA) are on their way to achieving that goal. Not only do they connect twelve traditional auctions in Belgium, the Netherlands, Northern Ireland, Scotland, England, and Denmark through the Internet, but they allow buyers anywhere in the world to monitor several of them simultaneously, receiving the same prices and product information as bidders in the halls. With this system, fishermen from the North Sea areas can sell easily to the markets of Spain and Italy, sometimes for 20 percent more than they would receive in their local markets. In addition, fishermen from Belgium and the Netherlands can bring their catch to the auctions in Scotland and England, closer to the rich Northern fishing grounds. Local ports benefit as well, since local fishermen can deliver the fish to the local docks and still reach the greater European market.

## Electronic Markets: Expanding Reach

In early marketplaces, all the essential tools of a transaction were close at hand: Customers could see the product, taste it, smell it, examine their options, judge the seller, pay for the goods, and even get satisfaction in the event of a dispute. Reputation, trust, and other intangibles were reinforced by the proximity of the participants.

Marketplaces had everything one could wish for but one: reach. Because the early markets were limited to the bourse house, the wharf, or another physical location, the number of traders was also limited. In fact, the marketplace could never grow much beyond the shouts of the auctioneers. That was the case for hundreds, even thousands, of years. Recent history has changed all that.

The catalyst for change has been communications technology. By moving trading processes from a single physical place to a virtual market space, new information technologies erase the need to be in one place. This lets a large number of people, spread across the globe, benefit from a new virtual closeness to supply and demand.

Beginning over two centuries ago, for instance, new information and communication technologies have continuously reshaped the New York Stock Exchange (NYSE).

| | |
|---|---|
| **1792** | Twenty-four brokers gather beneath a buttonwood tree in lower Manhattan. |
| **1817** | They establish a formal organization in a rented room at 40 Wall Street. |
| **1826** | Agents with flags relay stock prices from Manhattan to New Jersey. |
| **1844** | Telegraph is invented and installed in the exchange. |
| **1866** | Transatlantic cable is completed and trading data is sent to London. |
| **1867** | Stock ticker is invented, transmitting current prices to investors everywhere; installed on floor in 1868. |
| **1878** | First telephone is installed on the floor, two years after its invention. |
| **1881** | First annunciator boards are installed for paging members. |
| **1883** | First electric lights are installed. |
| **1903** | First pneumatic tubes are acquired. |
| **1930** | The 500-character-per-minute ticker, twice as fast as its predecessor, is introduced. |
| **1953** | First automated quotation service is introduced. |
| **1962** | First optical card readers are installed. |
| **1964** | The "900" ticker, nearly twice as fast as its predecessor, is introduced. |

**1966**    First radio pagers installed, replacing
            annunciator boards.

**1973**    Fully automated Designated Order Turnaround
            (DOT) system is introduced to route orders.

**1978**    Intermarket Trading System (ITS) electronically
            links all the exchanges.

**1984**    Launch of SuperDot 250, an electronic order-
            routing system that links member firms to
            specialists' posts on the trading floor.

**1994**    Integrated Technology Network permits the
            trading of more than 1 billion shares a day.

**1996**    Launch of real-time stock tickers on CNBC and
            CNN-FN.

**1997**    Wireless Data System is inaugurated, allowing
            brokers to send and retrieve information from
            any location on the trading floor.

**1999**    Opening of 3D Trading Floor, an advanced
            trading floor operations center.

**2000**    Launch of NYSE Direct+, providing immediate
            automatic execution of limit orders.[1]

The telegraph, telephone, and computer have had an
enormous impact on the New York Stock Exchange and
many other markets. The markets have grown from one circle of traders to millions of buyers and sellers who are connected to the Internet and can trade shares listed on the
NYSE with ease. To be sure, the NYSE still maintains a trading
floor. Likewise, human beings are still essential to ensure or-
derly and fair trading. But technology dramatically improves
the efficiency of trade processes internal to the exchange
and expands its reach to traders via the telephone and the
Internet.

The Nasdaq, a fully virtual market, pushes technology even farther. The Nasdaq consists of computer systems that broadcast the lowest offer and highest bid prices to more than 1.3 million users in 83 countries. Multiple Nasdaq market makers use this system to simultaneously buy and sell different stocks. Orders entered by market makers are matched against offers and executed as trades. When customers want to buy a Nasdaq stock, they call their broker or use their online brokerage account to specify the quantity, and choose either to buy it at the variable market price or enter a limit order specifying the price at which they are willing to buy the shares. The trade is executed when the Nasdaq system discovers a match and a market maker who is willing to sell the quantity of shares either at the market price or at the limit order price. Millions of individual investors can now trade shares efficiently by entering their orders online.

Improvements in telecommunications and information technologies reduce the market's dependence on place. Rapid computing and versatile communications systems allow buyers, sellers, and merchants to meet and transact in cyberspace rather than in a physical space. Few investors actually meet their stockbrokers anymore.

In a transformation similar to that of stock markets, the Internet is beginning to create virtual markets and market processes. It not only extends the "reach" of the markets, it extends their "richness" as well. In other words, the Internet not only is able to deliver market information and trading opportunities to more participants, but also provides a partial simulation of the physical marketplace itself. The Internet cannot completely simulate the full experience of a physical marketplace, of course. But in the future, new technologies will make the cyber experience more and more like the real thing.

Yet the transformation of markets from place to space is not simple. This chapter explains how information technologies are reshaping old markets and creating new ones. It defines the key market processes, examines the challenges and opportunities in transitioning each process from place to space, and explores the implications of this transition on the future of markets. Like Becaus-Pieters, some executives will recognize the opportunities and seize the value of electronic markets. Others will be forced to react to the inevitable emergence of new electronic markets—and the threat they pose to their supplier and distribution channels.

## Key Market Processes

Traditional and electronic markets both consist of a series of trading processes that create value for buyers and sellers. We have identified eleven key market processes, often traditionally located in close physical proximity, that must migrate partly or fully to cyberspace to make electronic markets successful. These activities, which we categorize as either basic trade processes or trade context processes, are listed below and shown in figure 2-1.[2]

The processes related directly to executing a trade of any kind include:

- Search processes that allow buyers and sellers to discover and compare trading opportunities

- Pricing processes to help buyers and sellers discover prices

- Logistics processes that coordinate the transfer of physical and digital goods between buyers and sellers

- Payment and settlement processes to transfer funds from buyer to seller

- Authentication processes to verify the quality of the goods sold and the credibility of the buyers and sellers

FIGURE 2-1

**Key Processes in Any Market**

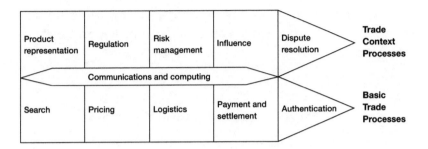

Five additional trade context processes enhance trust among trading parties and legitimize the trade. These include:

- Product representation processes that specify the presentation of products and services to buyers and sellers

- Regulation processes that record and recognize the transaction within a framework of laws and rules to signal it as legitimate and conforming to a set of market rules and social principles

- Risk management processes to reduce buyer and seller risks in a transaction

- Influence processes to ensure that commitments among trading partners are met

- Dispute resolution processes that resolve conflicts among buyers, sellers, and market makers such as auction houses

The communications and computing process enables integration of all other trading processes into specific markets for buyers and sellers. Thus, markets are a place, whether real or virtual, where these processes are available to support trading between buyers and sellers. The key challenge of electronic market makers is to successfully migrate existing ways of undertaking these processes from place to space. Next we examine how technology is transforming these fundamental market processes, creating opportunities, and posing challenges.

## Transforming Basic Trade Processes

Like traditional market makers, electronic market makers must get the basic trade processes right. This means they must:

1. Find the right buyers and sellers for the products being offered and bring them together in the marketplace.

2. Recognize the pricing advantages that exist in electronic markets and learn to use them effectively.

3. Recognize that shipping and logistics still mean moving molecules. (You can sell a fish in cyberspace, but you can't deliver it over a T-1 line.)

4. Familiarize themselves with the new ways to assure secure payment and settlement in cyberspace.

5. Authenticate the quality of the goods and services offered at a distance.

### Bringing Buyers and Sellers Together

In traditional markets, buyers may confront mounds of fish on the wharf or thousands of flowers in the flower halls. They are rarely overwhelmed by what is spread before them. However, this is not the case in electronic markets. Many of the electronic auction pioneers began with the promise that they would deliver more goods to the marketplace than had ever before been assembled in one place. And it was not just volume that they promised, but diversity. That promise, we've come to recognize, is fatally flawed.

If an electronic market is too big and too confusing, buyers and sellers will have difficulty finding the right deal. Some experts call this the plague of "information overload," where finding the proverbial needle in the haystack is not made easier by adding more hay. For online market makers, the moral is clear: If you plan to run a big cyber warehouse, be sure to engage the search tools that will help consumers find their way.

A good example of this is Bandwidth.com, a company formed in 1999 to sell and trade telecommunications and bandwidth capacity. At first, Bandwidth seemed to have it all: a vendor base of more than fifty-six telecommunications bandwidth suppliers and an Internet marketplace that could inexpensively permit traders, whether from Zimbabwe or Dallas, Texas, to buy and sell long-distance network services. The problem was that with all the various products and bandwidth offerings, customers had some 6 million product combinations to choose from. How could the company guide its customers to the kind of bandwidth and products they wanted, without overwhelming them with hundreds of thousands of alternatives?

Bandwidth took two important steps. First, it hired Perfect.com to customize a product that would help customers assign weightings to different product features, thereby guiding them to the products they wanted. This innovation alone helped the company double its revenues. But customers had to articulate and detail their preferences online using an unfamiliar process. So Bandwidth went a step further, hiring brokers to help the customers find what they wanted. The brokers not only helped the company raise revenues tenfold, they also contributed about 90 percent of revenues by late 2001. By understanding its market, its buyers' needs, and its sellers' needs, Bandwidth avoided becoming yet another dot-bomb.

The lessons from Bandwidth are clear. Despite the opportunity to reach new customers, transitioning markets from place to space is not as simple as putting up an online catalog. Transactions involving very complex and highly customized products may be fully automated someday (when tools emerge to help customers conveniently specify their preferences across multiple product attributes and configurations). But until then, such complex decisions are best supported by a combination of the best features of emerging technologies *and* the intelligence and problem-solving capabilities of smart service representatives.

## Pricing in the Electronic Market

In traditional markets, pricing is relatively easy. Market participants can haggle with each other directly or use an auction to reach a price. In the case of an auction, the rules for bidding are set. In the common English auction, for instance, people bid until the price goes no higher, at which time the item is sold to the highest bidder.

But both haggling and auctions are expensive in terms of time and opportunity costs to the participants. So a third alternative emerged—the posted offer (or static pricing). Here, the seller offers a fixed price to the buyer (typically production and distribution costs of the product plus a margin). Posted offers are common in supermarkets and retail stores. Unfortunately, even posted prices can be costly. To set or change the price of an item, say, in a supermarket, the store incurs a "menu cost." Given the low margin on many supermarket items, the store must avoid very frequent price changes that reduce margins to a loss.

Electronic markets and online catalogs have dramatically changed the dynamics of pricing. Not only can prices in an online market change frequently and with little cost, adding vitality to the market, but traders can bid in multiple pricing venues simultaneously, creating new opportunities for profit. Airlines, hotels, and industries that produce perishable goods, for instance, use dynamic pricing and yield management strategies to maximize their revenue.[3]

The Internet adds others twists to pricing. Consider Liquidation.com, the seller of surplus assets. In a traditional auction, all participants interested in a specific product must participate at the time the product is auctioned. In doing so, they must absorb opportunity costs (since they cannot be doing anything else at the time). But in Liquidation's auctions, bidders can program a software agent to bid on their behalf, raising the bid incrementally in competition until either the bidder wins or the agent reaches the bidder's maximum bid. In this case, the buyer can be doing something else and is relieved of time and opportunity costs.

Internet auctions have other advantages. In physical markets, for instance, the market maker can generally run only a few auctions simultaneously. In cyberspace, however, the market maker can replace the auctioneer with a software program, and offer hundreds or even thousands of simultaneous auctions (as is the case at eBay). Unconstrained by the costs of auctioneers and facilities, online auctions can also last more than a day. While traditional haggling has its time limits, electronic auctions can last indefinitely.

Pricing transparency is another impact of the transition from place to space, one in which both buyers and sellers can check the going prices during auctions, thereby helping them to set their bid and sell levels more accurately. We will speak more of this in chapter 7, but the result is that both buyers and sellers wind up leaving less money on the table.

## Coping with Logistics

Traditional marketplaces were set along major highways and trade routes. But as buyers, sellers, and products converged on one spot, logistics were always a problem. Consider a typical Dutch flower auction, for instance, where there might have been 2,500 trucks transporting produce, 2,000 buyers milling about, 60,000 auction clock transactions, and some 20,000 flower carts rattling through the auction halls on any day. Given the fragile nature of the product, transporting it to and from the auction halls could damage the product.

Online markets can solve this problem simply by decoupling the trading and product storage locations. When the Tele Flower auction (see chapter 1) began, for instance, the trading for the first time was done online, without the physical presence of traders. The flowers, meanwhile, were housed at a remote warehouse (rather than at the auction site). In the end, technology changed the face of the market, and both the traders and the flowers were fresher for it.

In other cases, however, logistics still bedevil an electronic market. Too often, online traders today forget that behind the cybertrading there are spoilable products—fish, vegetables, flowers—that must reach the buyers in good condition.

The Pan European Fish Auctions, for instance, initially left it up to the buyers to transport their fish southward from the Northern fishing grounds. But it soon became clear that only the big buyers with access to large transportation resources could participate. Subsequently, PEFA has helped all buyers by finding transportation vendors and negotiating preferred vendor arrangements with them. Small buyers are now able to participate. Without these critical transportation arrangements, PEFA could well have failed.

This was certainly the case in the failure of MetalSite, MetalSpectrum, Aluminium.com, and several other metal exchanges. Although there are many reasons for their failure—

the inherent size and competition in these markets to mention two—it was also caused by the high cost of transporting the metals and ores over long distances. Their weight alone limited the likely volume of metals and ores that could be traded. Limiting the effective geographic size of the market thus limited market competition and liquidity.

## Assuring Payment and Settlement in Cyberspace

Payment and settlement processes were among the first trade processes to transition from place to space. By the seventeenth century, traders increasingly bought goods through such new commercial instruments as letters of credit, promissory notes, and other paper-based documents. In this shift from bartered goods, which had been widely accepted, to money and commercial paper, the need arose for trusted third parties—banks and insurers. Long-distance trade was further expanded, thanks to the rise of the nation-state, which supported chartered companies and the modern corporation.

Banks were among the first to use telecommunications to transfer funds and increase the efficiency of payments and settlements. Indeed, existing infrastructures (from credit cards to the Society for Worldwide Interbank Financial Telecommunication [SWIFT] network) met many of the needs of buyers and sellers. The Internet, however, holds the potential to further reduce the transaction costs of payment and settlement. Part of the cost reduction will arise from better standards among banks for letters of credit and other trade documents.

Bolero.net, for instance, transmits letters of credit and other trade documents between banks and importers, exporters, and shipping organizations. Formed by a consortium of 6,700 financial institutions in 189 countries, therefore part-owned by SWIFT, and the TT Club, a mutual insurer for the freight transport industry, Bolero runs by a set of rules that all users are required to accept. Its electronic messaging standards simplify setting up and ensuring payments between traders. Identrus.com, another online player, is a global consortium of financial institutions that issues digital credentials and warranties against credential errors. These assurances, in turn, create the structure for electronic letters of credit and contracts, prequalified buyer credentials, and prequalified seller performance certificates.

As companies transition to electronic markets, they will benefit from increasingly efficient payment and settlement systems. But old methods will have to be continuously transformed for new settings. In the early days of the World Wide Web, a number of new payment and settlement systems were created, from CyberCash to DigiCash. Few of these systems added substantial value or convenience over credit cards. Today, as wireless phones become more prevalent, financial institutions are exploring their use for convenient wireless payments.

Mobile phones are perfectly suited for consumer transactions because they allow users to pay easily and with security. The SIM card in a mobile phone provides security and authenticates the user of the phone. As Digital Interactive Television emerges, payment and settlement systems will have to adapt to these new settings. The challenges for market makers will be to integrate new payment options into their markets and address the omnipresent threat of computer hacking, which forces companies to continually revisit the cutting edge in secure payments and settlements.

## Authenticating People, Goods, and Services

Payments are not the only aspect of online trading that require authentication. So do the qualities of the products that are on the block, the identity of the buyer or seller, and their capabilities to pay for or sell a product or service. In traditional physical markets, of course, the products were laid out before the buyers, the buyer and seller were present, and title to goods could be directly verified. But in cyberspace (and especially on vast public sites like eBay), buyers must rely on the seller or unknown third parties to authenticate the goods—or they must purchase on the basis of sheer trust, rather than verification.

The latter can be costly to the buyer and seller, as underscored by a recent report from the FBI's Internet Fraud Complaint Center (IFCC). It noted that online auctions accounted for 48.8% of fraud complaints, and nondelivery of goods ordered online came in second at 19.2%. (Third was securities fraud at 16.9% and fourth was credit card fraud at 4.8%.) The average monetary loss per complaint was $665. On the other hand, eBay has said that only one in 40,000 listings results in a fraud claim that is paid by its insurance company. eBay takes the problem very seriously, however, as its reputation is on the line.

Verifying the quality and authenticity of goods being traded is no easy task. It can also affect the price of the trade. In 1970, George Akerlof (winner of the 2001 Nobel Prize in economics) wrote a classic paper on why used cars are sold at a substantial discount to the price of a new car.[4] In the paper, Akerlof noted that the used-car buyer does not know if the car is a "lemon," that is, if it has hidden defects that they might detect only after purchase. To avoid this, the buyer can hire a mechanic to check out the car. But this is a somewhat costly and imperfect solution. So, buyers mitigate this risk by discounting the price they are willing to pay. Many states in the U.S. now have "lemon laws" to protect the consumer if they discover such a hidden flaw, but remedying the problem can still be costly.

Online market makers can take several steps to address these authentication problems. First, they can provide inspection services, either directly or by using trusted third parties, to authenticate the quality of the goods traded. Aucnet, a Japanese online used-car auction, does this to reassure buyers—and earns sellers higher prices for it. Second, market makers can also work with trusted third parties to provide services such as public key encryption and certification authorities to verify market participants are who they say they are (see "The Role of Public Key Encryption"). Finally, they can also link to services such as credit checks from Equifax or provide title searches for various goods.

In summary, while there are limits, new information technologies have improved the efficiency and reach of basic trade processes such that traders no longer must converge on a physical market. Sometimes the technological innovation exceeds the customer's ability to absorb the new technology, as at Bandwidth. But as technology costs fall and systems improve, many new efficiencies can be expected to reduce basic trade process costs even further.

## Transforming Trade Context Processes

Markets, whether physical or virtual, are meeting places where economic activity takes place in a broad social context. Trading is ultimately a social activity, one in which both buyers and sellers want to feel that a fair and equitable outcome awaits them. The trade context processes, therefore, support the creation and maintenance of trust and confidence. To paraphrase Ken Arrow, the Nobel laureate economist, "Trust reduces the frictions in commerce."[5] Trust is the willingness of a buyer or seller to rely on the other with confidence, that is, to believe the other will fulfill his or her obligations.

Many factors can increase or decrease trust in a marketplace. These include prior reputations of the buyer or seller;

## THE ROLE OF PUBLIC KEY ENCRYPTION

Public key encryption has made possible a range of third-party services for authentication. In public key encryption, two matched keys are issued to individuals or businesses—a public key published to all and a private key kept private by the individuals or businesses. Messages encrypted by a specific private key can be opened only by the matching public key and vice versa. This can be used to create a web of trust to authenticate the identities of businesses or individuals who have otherwise never met or transacted.

The American Bankers Association (ABA), for instance, has created its TrustID program, under which the ABA issues guidelines allowing member banks to issue TrustID digital certificates to their customers. Here the member bank becomes a certificate authority, verifying the identity of an individual or a business and issuing them a digital certificate. This digital certificate includes information such as identifying information (name, address, etc.), the person's public key (so recipients can verify messages encrypted with the sender's private key), dates of certificate validity, and issuer information.

Once the TrustID certificate is issued to individuals or businesses and signed by the bank's private key, owners of the certificates can trade with each other without having to meet. If a sender sends an encrypted message to a recipient with a TrustID, the recipient can use the bank's public key that is published to open the certificate and verify its authenticity. Next, the sender's public key, which is sent in the certificate, can "unlock" the message from the sender. Such electronic documents can thereby substitute for paper contracts, signed face-to-face.

the assurances provided by third parties in the market space, such as certificate authorities, independent appraisers, and the Better Business Bureau; and favorable prior experiences with the buyer or seller. The greater the trust, the more willing the buyer and seller are to cooperate, meet each other's needs, and execute trades without resorting to expensive contingent contracts.

In transitioning trade context processes from place to space, market makers must rethink how they:

1.  Represent offers effectively when you can't see, touch, or smell them.

2.  Regulate the market to maintain trust when the market can encompass the entire world.

3.  Reduce the trading risks confronted by buyers *and* sellers.

4.  Influence the behaviors of market participants to conform to the norms of the marketplace.

5.  Resolve disputes in cyberspace.

### Representing Molecules Using Bits

How do you convey the beauty of a flower in cyberspace? In the Dutch flower markets, online bidders must rely on written descriptions, augmented by a sometimes-grainy digital photograph. Compared with the flood of sensations that one experiences when viewing a flower up close, cyberspace has a long way to go.

Although this weakness has hurt many online markets, the gap is slowly closing. Aerome AG, for instance, is building hardware and software technologies to reproduce and convey smells to computer users.[6] Similarly, Immersion Technologies has created a computer mouse that conveys touch. With Immersion's Touchsense technology, for example, you can feel the texture of a fabric before purchasing it. This is only the beginning. In twenty-five years, we may be surprised by what we can experience on our computer screens.

But the real action in product representation today is Extensible Markup Language (XML). XML may not help customers touch and smell a rose. But through its ability to add layers of information to product descriptions, it will help customers identify what they want more closely than ever before. (See "What Is XML?") XML is already being used worldwide. RosettaNet, for instance, a consortium of some 400 of the world's leading information technology, electronic, and semiconductor companies, is setting up open e-business process standards using XML.[7] RosettaNet provides dictionaries with definitions, exchange protocols, and so-called Partner Interface Processes that make online trading easier.

Companies are excited about XML for the same reason that they were enthusiastic about the advent of Electronic Data Interchange (EDI) several years ago. Just as EDI created efficiency in trading between companies, XML lets them specify business rules and automatically process orders and other information. Furthermore, XML standards will allow companies to use software not only to search the markets for good deals, but to trade automatically on their behalf.

## Regulating Market Activity

Regulation is the other side of the "free market" coin. The most advanced free market systems, in fact, also have the most advanced regulatory systems. These systems establish common ground and rules of conduct for all market participants, easing the "friction" of trading and enhancing confidence in the fairness of the exchange. The Securities and Exchange Commission regulates the U.S. stock exchanges, for instance, ensuring the uniform disclosure of corporate

## WHAT IS XML?

Hypertext Markup Language (HTML) is the protocol that has become the predominant tool for designing electronic interfaces.[8] Most Web pages are constructed using HTML. In the example below, the HTML tells the computer what words should be underlined.

<UL>$2344.00, Laptop Computer Notebook with
Enhanced Keyboard </UL>

The problem with HTML is that the tags convey little meaning other than formatting. In contrast, Extensible Markup Language, or XML, not only enriches descriptions of materials but also provides a common language and shared syntax that can be used for many purposes—for instance, trading goods automatically between organizations.[9] XML codes information with semantic tags. This enables software agents to process the information and automatically execute embedded business rules that lead to inventory replenishment or trades between companies. Meaningful annotation is, in essence, what XML is all about. In XML we would write the item details as follows.

<ItemDetail>

<UnitPrice>

<Money currency="USD">2344.00</Money>

</UnitPrice>

<Description xml:lang="en">Laptop Computer
Notebook</Description>

<UnitOfMeasure>EA</UnitOfMeasure>

<Classification
domain="UNSPSC">43171801</Classification>

```
<URL>http://www.supplier.com/Punchout.asp</URL>

<Extrinsic name="ExtDescription">Enhanced
keyboard</Extrinsic>

</ItemDetail>
```

As we can see, the XML specification provides far more detail about the item and its attributes. Computers can process information more easily in XML than HTML. First, computers can automatically apply rules to convert the XML representation into HTML code for display on a Web browser. Second, information can be more easily shifted into databases, with data shifted into the correct fields for price, product, etc. Third, the semantic tags make it easier to understand and process data from XML documents than from HTML—for example, to run software that converts price data from U.S. dollars into Japanese yen.

information and watching for such illegal activities as insider trading.

As new electronic markets arise, the market makers or industry organizations themselves often must build the rules of conduct. eBay, for instance, has had problems with shill bidding (in which sellers utilize phantom buyers to inflate bid prices). When eBay, through monitoring, discovers such unethical trading activity, it gives first offenders a thirty-day suspension, and repeat offenders are permanently banned from the market. Regulating markets is challenging when markets cross judicial and geographic borders and as electronic markets become more complex. Often technical innovation in markets outruns consensus on the principles of regulating them. But failures in (self-)regulation can be very costly, as exemplified by Enron in December 2001. We discuss Enron further in chapter 6.

## Managing Online Trading Risks

Risk management services insure transactions and provide information to help the buyer and seller deal with price, delivery, theft, and other risks. As e-commerce proliferates, a number of insurance companies are beginning to offer insurance services to mitigate these risks. Similarly, many credit card companies limit consumer liability for online fraudulent credit card use.

Risk mitigation for buyers and sellers is often achieved through third-party services, which are linked to the trading site. For example, From2.com—acquired in March 2000 by Arzoon—assesses and insures shipping risks. Similarly, Tradecard.com provides insurance for international freight. Escrow services also facilitate trade at a distance. Escrow.com, for example, intermediates electronic market transactions before payments are released to the seller to ensure that a satisfactory product is delivered. As online trading expands, the risks to both buyer and seller must be met through the expansion of such services.

## Influencing Online and Offline Behaviors

Rules are meaningless if they cannot be enforced or if market participants cannot be influenced to conform to them. One way in which electronic auctions have succeeded in regulating their participants is through feedback, in which buyers and sellers rate and post comments about each other. The comments typically describe the particular transaction as well as the registered user. In most cases, customers will avoid sellers with bad ratings and reputations.

Business-to-business commerce uses similar rating systems. For instance, Open Ratings, an online service partnering with Dun & Bradstreet, asks purchasers for feedback on their experiences with particular vendors and rates them according to the speed of delivery, the quality of services, and the integrity of the products themselves. The information is aggregated so that buyers can compare the performance of multiple vendors. Not only does the information help buyers, but it provides an incentive for sellers to meet commitments and behave ethically. Market makers can also suspend buyers and sellers who don't follow the rules and deny them future trading rights. Such rights of exclusion are practiced by markets ranging from eBay to Nasdaq.

## Facilitating Dispute Resolution

Efficient dispute-resolution mechanisms also reduce the costs of market participation. Generally, disputants can resolve their problems through direct negotiation or through lawsuits and third-party interventions. A number of third-party services are emerging to support online dispute resolution. Settle Online, for instance, provides confidential Internet-based dispute-resolution services. SquareTrade provides an online arbitration service.

Some markets also establish their own in-house dispute-resolution mechanisms to avoid the high costs of court-ordered resolutions. As electronic markets proliferate and transcend traditional legal jurisdictions, however, market makers will need to develop more complicated dispute-resolution systems, ones that can be enforced as efficiently as those in courts of law.

As market makers transition from place to space, they have to design new trade context processes appropriate to cyberspace. In contrast to basic trade processes, which are rapidly improved by technological innovations, trade context processes are transformed more slowly by technology. Indeed, new trade context processes require broad social consensus among participants for successful adoption, from a new XML specification of a messaging standard to market rules that set behavioral norms. This need for social consensus makes changes in these processes more difficult and leads to slower adoption than changes in basic trade processes.

## From Virtual Processes to Decentralized Markets

The transition from place to space makes it possible for core market processes to be decentralized. No longer do market processes, such as logistics and pricing, have to be co-located. Instead, thanks to efficient communications and computing processes, they can be decentralized.

The decentralization of markets follows the overall decentralization of computing and communications capabilities that has occurred over the last decade. Traditional phone systems, for example, began as a hierarchical system, one with a central office and trunk switches. Hierarchies were great at conserving scarce intelligence and bandwidth. As LANs (local area networks) emerged, they formed a new "peer-to-peer" communications architecture, one in which routing was not centralized. Rather, every personal computer connected to a LAN was a repository of intelligence, listening for relevant messages on the shared communications pipeline. Similarly, in peer-to-peer computer architecture, individual computers in a network interact without the need for a central server or "hub." In the most decentralized markets, similarly, trading applications interact directly, without having to go through a centralized hub.

The Nasdaq market and emerging Electronic Communications Networks, or ECNs, are examples. The Nasdaq computer systems broadcast the lowest offers and highest bids to more than 360,000 terminals, and orders entered by market makers are matched against offers and executed as trades. Meanwhile, the advent of ECNs, which were started in 1997 to increase competition among the exchanges, enables an even more decentralized form of trading. ECNs are electronic communications applications that allow participants to trade shares directly, without having to use the services of Nasdaq market makers.

ECNs give members new flexibility in directly negotiating prices and spreads. ECNs also route orders not directly fulfilled within the ECN network to the Nasdaq system, thus taking advantage of the availability of market markers. ECN networks have proliferated rapidly and now account for 35 percent of all trading in Nasdaq-listed stocks. Examples of ECNs include Instinet, Island, Bloomberg Tradebook, and Archipelago. The shift of trading away from the Nasdaq reduces the spreads and profit opportunities available to traditional Nasdaq market makers.

Naturally this has not gone unnoticed, and traditional market makers have been complaining about the fragmentation of markets as well as the challenges posed to customers, who now must comb multiple ECNs and the Nasdaq to find the best price. As traditional market makers lose market share, they are calling for a centralized system to record all limit orders across networks, allowing market makers to see all orders and thus compete more effectively with ECNs. As a result, technology-enabled decentralization can have major impacts on where transactions are conducted and who can profit from market making.

Driven by the peer-to-peer model, some market software providers like Netrana are breaking from the centralized B2B model. The primary characteristic of such markets is the elimination of the centralized intermediary. In its place, traders post their bids on the Internet, using peer-to-peer software that communicates to other traders. When matches in prices, quantities, and other details are reached, the trades are made. Advocates of such structures note that since the middleman is eliminated, the costs are lower.

Although peer-to-peer markets may increase in the future, pure forms of these models are likely to be rare. For one, they will probably work only where the trading parties have already established trust and a long trading history. Furthermore, peer-to-peer will succeed only in situations where the peers have agreed on such critical functions as authentication and logistics. They will also have to agree on directory services (so that peers can find each other), standards for interconnection to legacy applications, security, and regulation to remedy breaches of trust. For these reasons, we expect that peer-to-peer will be most usefully employed as independent components—specializing in auction services and other market processes—as they are built into the more conventional electronic markets.

## Navigating the Changes

Managers will need the courage and imagination shown by Marie Becaus-Pieters to seize the opportunities and address the challenges of new information technologies. Above all, new market makers must transition the various market processes from place to space. Like Bandwidth's managers, they will need to find the right balance between humans and computers.

Redesigning trade processes, after all, is not just a matter of technical implementation of new market processes. It's also a matter of determining how market participants can create and maintain a community of trust in a detached and decentralized cyberspace environment.

In chapter 3 we will turn to the big issues facing market designers: finding ways to provide value to *all* participants and achieving liquidity quickly. We will also provide a framework for addressing process changes.

# 3

---

# Making Markets Work

IN THE PAST, when mutual fund managers prepared for a big trade, word would inevitably leak out onto the street. Brokers, hedge fund managers, market makers, and day traders would all join the action, pushing up the cost of large-cap stock trades by about 1 percent and small-cap transactions by as much as 4.5 percent. Some fund managers tried to mask their intent by breaking up their orders, filling them gradually. But in most cases it didn't work—the market recognized the "footprint" that identified who was about to make the trade and then reacted to its best advantage.

Several new market makers have come up with solutions. HarborsidePlus, for instance, developed a trading system that essentially wipes out the "footprint" that signals a big trade.[1] HarborsidePlus works by taking "snapshots" of its members' trade blotters and feeding them into a central server. The server then sends out a list of possible big block trades to all the members—without revealing names. When a match is found, the server automatically alerts the two parties about the opportunity.

But HarborsidePlus doesn't rely solely on technology to complete the deal. Indeed, once the two parties are found via the server, HarborsidePlus has a trader call each of them. The anonymity of the players is maintained, and hopefully the deal is struck. In this way, HarborsidePlus has not only found a high-tech solution to the problem, but also maintained the old-fashioned sense of human contact. Best of all, the HarborsidePlus exchange has reduced the cost of big trades from about five cents per share to around two cents.

HarborsidePlus is not alone in creating value in a new market. Consider 12Snap, a new auction site where traders use their cell phones to make trades. Once a customer signs up with 12Snap, they begin receiving items for sale with a starting price. If they accept the offer, they call back. As the bidding drives the prices higher, they receive updates on the phone screen. To bid higher, they must keep calling back.

But 12Snap doesn't auction off everyday items. Rather, it has found its niche in entertainment: rides in a hot air balloon; a new Sony Playstation; a famous chef's three-star dinner, delivered to your home; even a date with a Playboy playmate. "We realized that the people using 12Snap—mostly between fourteen and twenty-eight years old—didn't really want theater tickets, stock reports, and such," says Cyriac Roeding, one of the company's founders. "They see the mobile phone as an entertainment device, and they wanted to have some fun with it." 12Snap has been a huge success, with its revenues drawn not only from the auctions, but from a percentage of the cellular calls as well.

## The Two Imperatives: Value and Liquidity

HarborsidePlus, 12Snap, and the Tele Flower Auction discussed in chapter 1 illustrate the first key imperative of building a successful electronic market: The market maker must create something of real *value*—a better value, certainly, than what the traditional market can offer. In the case of HarborsidePlus, the value proposition is clearly the anonymity that allows mutual fund managers (and other institutional investors) to trade without revealing their hand. For 12Snap, it's the recognition that young people use their cell phones for entertainment—and that's what they want a cell phone auction to reflect. Finally, the TFA improved access for East African flower growers and vastly simplified the logistics of flower auctions, making remote bidding not only possible but attractive. In each case, these successful ventures were able to instill value into their operations.

All three illustrate another important imperative: The market must have *liquidity*—enough players to make the market work. Fortunately, in the case of HarborsidePlus, the benefits of its system were great enough that a market quickly formed around the core idea. The same was true of 12Snap and the TFA.

In the next section we build on the importance of value and liquidity with three other illustrative stories. But these will be different—all three of these initiatives failed. In the rest of the chapter we discuss how to build value by challenging the status quo, improving basic trade processes, and reaching a critical mass quickly. Finally, we describe a framework for action—one that can help managers identify the best opportunities and strategies.

## Creating Compelling Value: A Tough Formula

When online markets began, the value proposition seemed simple and straightforward; it was the use of the Internet itself. But now we recognize that taking markets from place to space is not easy. Too often, the value proposition gets lost along the way.

Consider the Vidifleur initiative, which was launched by FloraHolland.[2] By 1990, FloraHolland was finding that the physical limitations of their auction facilities constrained their growth. They needed to reduce the logistical requirements for running their auctions. The idea was to use video auctioning to allow buyers to trade from outside the auction hall, thereby uncoupling valuation and logistics. When the flowers or plants arrived at the auction hall in Naaldwijk, a photograph was taken, digitized, and stored in auction computers. The computer transferred the picture for display to a screen in the auction hall, where buyers could bid for the product based on the image of the product.

Buyers were also able to see and bid for the potted plants via computer screens in their private offices; they could even see a synchronized representation of the official clock in the auction hall. Considering that the market auctioned off millions of flowers and potted plants every day, the new technology seemed to be a significant step forward.

But buyers didn't agree. First, they complained that the quality of the video images was poor. Second, the system provided no efficiencies for the buyers—in fact, they said they lost advantage by not being physically present in the hall. (See "The Beauty of Body Language.") At the back of each auction hall is a coffee shop where buyers interact informally and share information about the market. Those trading from a private office missed the social interaction and the information that existed for those who were on location.

In particular, individuals who were on location were able to read the faces of the other bidders, thereby gauging the interest they had for particular auctions and products. They could *feel* the bidding in a way that those outside the hall could not. Those watching a computer screen in private offices could not observe the reactions of other buyers to the bidding process. Thus, information asymmetries were created between those on the floor and those participating remotely. Before long, these complaints led to the failure of the Vidifleur auction.

Vidifleur wasn't the only electronic flower auction to lose its bloom. Consider another failure: The Aalsmeer Flower Auction began a sample-based auction for trading potted plants.[3] In this case, the grower would send a sample of the product to the auction house, along with information on the

**THE BEAUTY OF BODY LANGUAGE**

When transitioning from place to space, market makers must be careful not to destroy value to participants through the loss of critical decision-making information. In well-established physical markets, the identities of buyers and their affiliations are clear. If there is an ongoing community of bidders, they become familiar with each other's body language and track other nonprice signals as they make pricing decisions. One can easily sense panic in a physical market, for instance. Thus, electronic markets have a problem. How can they replicate the important physical signals that steer most traditional markets?

Business economists Joshua Coval and Tyler Shumway analyzed the information content and impacts of the ambient noise level in the Chicago Board of Trade's thirty-year treasury bond futures trading pit.[4] This trading pit uses the open-outcry exchange, where traders stand in a large pit and bark out the prices and quantities at which they are willing to buy and sell. Until recently, this system was the undisputed mechanism for allowing many individuals to concurrently trade large volumes of a given futures contract.

Coval and Shumway measured the sound level in the pit—what traders commonly refer to as the "buzz"—for two months. In the pit are more than 400 participants. Controlling for a variety of other variables, including lagged price changes, trading volumes, and news announcements, they found that the sound level conveys information that is highly significant both economically and statistically. Changes in the sound level forecast the volatility of prices and a number of other market characteristics.

This study clearly showed that nontransaction information such as the ambient noise levels conveyed signals that helped traders predict future market conditions, including price volatility, the depth of the market, and trade composition. Clearly, the "buzz" was more than just noise. Those leading the transition from place to space must account for the information losses or gains that may impact the pricing process—or risk the failure of electronic market initiatives.

Although electronic markets may not be able to replicate all the information and "buzz" of a physical marketplace, electronic market makers must make sure that the same information is available to all participants. They can even create other communication mechanisms and signals, such as message boards, to capture information about how participants feel about the market. Preventing information asymmetries and making more market information available to all participants is critical to creating and maintaining trust in the market.

available inventory, packaging alternatives, and delivery constraints. During the auction, the sample would represent the entire inventory available to buyers.

All of the information was exchanged with the grower through electronic data interchange (EDI). By reducing the number of times the flowers were handled, sample-based auctioning was designed to reduce the costs due to transportation, packaging, and damage. The participants— the growers, the buyers, and the auction house—expected a number of different benefits. First, by uncoupling logistics and price determination, the auction house and the growers expected to increase the number of transactions per hour. In reality, however, the number of transactions per hour decreased because buyers had to specify the terms of delivery.

Second, although the auction house expected 45 percent of the supply of potted plants to be sold via the sample-based auction, the actual figure was only 10 percent. Thus, sample-based auctioning did not effectively reduce storage requirements. After numerous attempts to increase the volume of sales transacted by sample-based auctions, they were discontinued in late 1994, a life span of only nine months.

Although the video-based and sample-based auctions provided a compelling value proposition to the auctioneer, neither provided significant advantages to the buyer and supplier, and thus both failed. The primary benefits to solving the logistics problems in these auctions accrued only to the auctioneer.

It is vital, then, for any market maker to carefully examine the allocations of benefits and costs as they are distributed to all stakeholders (buyers, suppliers, and market makers). Whenever someone is left worse off by the change to electronic markets, it is unlikely a new market will succeed, unless that party is initially subsidized or faces competitive pressures to participate in the market.

## Exmtrade: A Failure in Apparel

It's not just flower auctions that have failed. Exmtrade, created by three senior executives from the apparel industry, is another.[5] Exmtrade's objective was to create an electronic market for trading excess merchandise in the apparel industry. In 1996, the company created proprietary software that allowed both manufacturers and retailers to display photographs of apparel, inventory holdings, and other information online.

In the apparel industry, major retailers typically carry the current fashions, while off-price retailers sell the late excess inventory. Because the manufacturing and merchandising components are fragmented, the supply chains often carry excess inventory. When this inventory is not cleared, it loses substantial value. Exmtrade's value proposition was to create an efficient marketplace, one that enabled large retailers and manufacturers to clear their merchandise in a centralized electronic market to off-price, discount retailers.

After developing the software, the company introduced it at various trade shows, where it was instantly recognized as an innovative product. Manufacturers and buyers took and installed thousands of copies of the software. Yet despite the warm reception at the shows and high installation and registration rates, few companies were actually using the software to clear excess merchandise. That meant little inventory on the site, which, in turn, discouraged buyers from going there. Surprised and dismayed, the executive team called a meeting with one of this book's authors to diagnose the problem.

The problem, it turned out, was that the merchandise suppliers were unable to master the new process of accessing the online marketplace, arranging the digital photographs of their products, and loading the information online. The process might not seem difficult, but it was novel, and it required suppliers to make changes in their organizations as well as retrain their personnel.

The company was left with two alternatives. The first was to establish a physical presence in a number of cities or, alternatively, have the suppliers mail samples of their goods to a central location, where they would be digitally photographed and then returned to the supplier. But this was also a major change in the habits of the suppliers.

The second, more radical alternative was to buy the merchandise from the suppliers very cheaply, assume the inventory risk, and then resell it online themselves. This would constitute a further risk, however, and would require substantial infrastructure. After evaluating the alternatives, the general partners chose the safest route: They decided to close Exmtrade.

Exmtrade could have been a win-win for all parties. Yet it failed because suppliers were reluctant to commit to a new technology until other suppliers were there first. It was a failure of the chicken-and-egg variety, and, in the end, Exmtrade never achieved sufficient value or volume, because no one considered the costs of new product representation methods and the changes in routine to suppliers. The result was that suppliers didn't put enough inventory for sale on the system, diminishing the interest of buyers and leading to the failure of the market initiative.

## The Two Hurdles to Value

What do Vidifleur, Aalsmeer Flower Auction's sample-based auction, and Exmtrade have to teach us? That at least two hurdles must be cleared in order for managers to create value.

First, new electronic markets challenge the status quo and the existing relationships between buyers and sellers. For a new model of trading to succeed, there must be buy-in from all parties—in other words, the new auction or electronic market must create a compelling value proposition for buyers, sellers, and market makers. This is the minimum condition for change.

Second, new market mechanisms must at minimum improve some or all of the basic trade processes. Since buyers and sellers don't want to spend much time searching or bargaining, improving the efficiency of basic trade processes (such as search, pricing, and authentication) creates substantial value. These process improvements can lower search and authentication costs for buyers and raise the price paid to sellers by decreasing the buyer's risk. If all players are better off, a new market has a good chance of succeeding. If someone is left out, it does not. TFA understood this: Its auction was carefully designed to assure there were no differences in the information available from the auction house to any buyer. This ensured fairness to all participants.

As electronic procurement auctions proliferate, some argue that a "win-win-win" among buyers, sellers, and market makers is not necessary—that buyer aggregation in these exchanges will force suppliers to participate for even lower margins. We expect that suppliers will trade through a variety of mechanisms, from electronic auctions to fixed long-term contracts, and that suppliers will make the best trade-offs available between reductions in margins and expanded volumes through access to new markets.

### Aucnet: Success with Used Cars

For an example of a market that meets both criteria—challenging the status quo and improving the basic trade process—look no farther than Japan's Aucnet.[6]

Aucnet is an online used-car market for car dealers that relies on three innovations: video images, character-based data, and a standardized inspector rating. It was started in Japan in 1985 and has been a hit ever since. The system works this way: The sellers must have their vehicles inspected by Aucnet mechanics, who assess damage and then rank the quality in a single number (from 1 to 10).

During the electronic auction, the seller and potential buyers are linked to Aucnet's central host computer via satellite connections. A car sold through Aucnet remains at the seller's location until the transaction is completed. Then a transport company delivers it directly to the buyer.

The advantage for car dealers is that Aucnet offers them the same information as conventional automobile auctions, but in much less time. Furthermore, the dealers don't have to spend a whole day at an auction in order to bid for the one or two cars they are interested in. Aucnet distributes its auction schedule in advance, so used-car dealers can download the data and images and make their choices. They can also use the information to gauge customer interest before they bid.

There's another side to Aucnet. Aucnet has done for cars what TFA did for flowers: create new value by authenticating quality. Aucnet consolidates quality control and authentication in their teams of mechanics, who inspect each car and give it a rating based on its merits.

Furthermore, by not requiring dedicated space for inventory (cars stay with the seller), Aucnet can easily accommodate its 15 percent yearly sales volume increases. In traditional auto auctions, 45 percent of the cars are typically unsold and have to be moved off the lot. On Aucnet, there are no cars to move. Little wonder, then, that by moving from place to space, Aucnet has created the largest auto auction in Japan. In 1995 it listed over 230,000 used cars. In 2001, it listed almost 390,000.

## Achieve Critical Mass Quickly

As we noted earlier, new electronic market and auction initiatives must quickly achieve critical mass and market liquidity. Electronic markets and auctions become more valuable as more and more traders participate. Economists refer to the extra benefit from an added participant that accrues to all other participants as a "positive externality." Once there are enough users to form a critical mass, most other users are likely to adopt the market quickly because of positive externalities, creating exponential growth.

On the other hand, if critical mass is not achieved quickly, the early adopters who expected to benefit from the addition of other participants are likely to abandon the market for other trading forums, causing the new market to fail. Two basic strategies are available to reach critical mass: subsidize early users and increase the cost of older transaction options.

### Subsidize Early User Adoption of the Market

Subsidizing early users is one way to drive a market quickly to critical mass. It may take only a few key buyers, attracted by steep discounts, to motivate other sellers to join. For this reason, markets should select the dominant suppliers and buyers as targets for subsidies. They create the greatest positive externalities, accelerating adoption by others. The Tele Flower Auction, for example, encourages growers and buyers to trade online by renting or even buying computers for them.

Alternatively, new markets may want to have a dominant buyer as a strategic investor. This creates commitment from the buyer. For example, Tapestria—an electronic market for fine interior fabrics that enables interior designers to purchase fabrics directly from the world's most prestigious mills—was created and supported by Hunter Douglas, the world leader in window coverings and a major manufacturer of architectural products. Hunter Douglas's initial investment of $25 million and its global strengths helped bring Tapestria to a point of competitive advantage.

New markets may also want to offer part of the service free to attract customers. PartMiner, as we noted in chapter 1, initially gave its CAPX database of product information free to users of its site, making its money on the brokerage of hard-to-find products. HarborsidePlus has reduced its transaction fees for early adopters.

OptiMark, on the other hand, suffered from a different critical mass problem: By the time its anonymous trade matching system, designed to improve market liquidity, was implemented two years after the project started, trading volumes had increased to such an extent in the existing market, it was much more liquid on its own. By then, traders didn't feel that OptiMark's system made much difference.

### Increase the Cost of Alternative Transaction Mechanisms

Although increasing the cost of certain options is rarely feasible in a competitive marketplace, many governments and communication monopolies have used this strategy successfully to get parties to switch from one technology to another.

France Telecom, for example, was able to assist the launch of its Minitel system by increasing the cost of traditional paper phone directories. For a crucial start-up period, French telephone users subscribing to Minitel could receive directory information such as telephone numbers and addresses only via their Minitel system. During this time, no paper-based telephone books were even provided.[7]

## One Step at a Time

Beyond these subsidy and penalty strategies, market makers must evaluate their strategy for diversifying their markets. It is important to achieve a critical mass in a particular market segment before diversifying to other segments. Without these considerations, one risks the same tale of failure that was the fate of a company called Nets Inc.

Nets Inc. began in 1990, the fifth start-up of entrepreneur Donald Jones. The company was an attempt to bring together regional buyers and sellers of manufacturing equipment. Originally called Automation News Network, the company printed monthly magazines of industry news and, every six months, produced an industrial directory diskette. Jones intended his paper and disk products to be a starting point; the goal would be a kind of electronic clearinghouse for manufacturing news and products.

With the development of the World Wide Web, Jones immediately saw that it could do everything he had hoped to do with a proprietary system, at a fraction of the cost. By the end of 1995, he had changed the name of his company to Industry.Net and had posted much of the information from his print catalogs and diskettes on the Web. Jones knew that the next step—moving from Internet publishing to Internet commerce—would require a serious infusion of capital.

The capital arrived in 1996 along with Jim Manzi, the former CEO of Lotus Development Corporation. Manzi was named CEO, and the name of the company was changed from Industry.Net to Nets Inc. The new company's goal was to improve the efficiency of business-to-business trading by creating catalogs across multiple markets and providing trading systems through auctions.

Nets Inc., however, failed to take off and was sold in 1997 at a substantial discount to Perot Systems.

Why did Nets Inc. fail? While there were many reasons, one worth noting was its rapid entry into multiple markets without building sufficient critical mass in any one market. In an electronic market, failure to achieve critical mass rapidly can be fatal. If suppliers don't see enough buyers for their product, or buyers don't see enough suppliers for their needs, both parties are likely to opt out. Nets Inc. assumed that a common set of product categories and market mechanisms could be developed across industries, although, for example, guidelines such as the electronic data interchange standards showed this was difficult to achieve. Nets Inc. also assumed that they could create substantial changes in how multiple industries did business, which, in the past, has been done only by powerful customers.

The moral here is that new markets and segments must be entered sequentially, with care taken to achieve critical mass in one market before addressing the next. Aucnet successfully executed this strategy. Aucnet got into used cars in 1985. Eight years later it started auctioning motorcycles. Then, in 1998, Aucnet started a satellite-linked flower auction, connecting growers and agricultural cooperatives with wholesalers and retailers. In July 2000 it expanded from one to two satellite channels. In 1999 Aucnet started the biggest watch auction site in Japan, where watches are inspected, appraised, and graded by Seiji Honma, Japan's leading watch repair expert. The range of merchandise has increased gradually from watches to jewelry, cigarette lighters, and cameras. In every new segment, Aucnet developed a strong partnership with established players, improving its likelihood of success even further.

## Reduce Transition Risk and Effort

To succeed, market makers should make transitioning to their service as risk-free as possible. These are the required steps:

- Increase trust in their product value through strict quality control.

- Adopt standards to reduce risks of technology obsolescence and integration.

- Design systems that integrate easily with existing procurement systems and software.

- Leverage existing providers of key market processes.

- Manage against technology failures.

Since an online market may be replacing one in which the buyer directly sought the vendor and the product, the new market must win the buyers' confidence. Strict product quality controls (like those at the TFA and Aucnet) can enhance buyer confidence by preinspecting the products before purchase. This is especially valuable for nonstandard products or those that can vary highly in quality. Indeed, as illustrated by Aucnet, reliable quality ratings can even boost prices.

Conforming to technological standards is a second strategy for reducing transition risks. For instance, developing online trading systems consistent with open Internet standards such as Extensible Markup Language (XML), rather than with a specialized semantic markup language, enhances the confidence of the new adopter that the technology will be supported, and that others will find it easy to participate.

New market makers must also be aware of the need to integrate their market mechanisms with the selling and buying processes of their suppliers and buyers. By designing systems that integrate new market processes with existing business processes, market makers are likely to avoid the pitfalls encountered by Exmtrade. This is particularly true as companies increasingly deploy enterprise resource planning systems.

Similarly, it's important to keep the processes of new markets as familiar to the participants as possible. HarborsidePlus, for instance, kept human beings in their process, supplementing its technological innovations. But some startups haven't. LiquidNet, a HarborsidePlus competitor, may have changed the process too much. It uses negotiation via instant messaging, which may be considered an improvement by some traders. But it is well known in the industry that people are more likely to drop trades when they face an anonymous instant messaging screen instead of a live person on the phone to whom they owe an explanation. Also, the technology requirements of instant messaging are more than some traders feel comfortable with. OptiMark, the first company to try anonymous matching through technology, did little to improve trade processes—in fact, data entry requirements shot up enormously, and traders saw no benefit in the process change. It increased their workload and the probability of errors. OptiMark has abandoned the system.

Today, third parties can reduce the cost of building and transitioning to electronic markets. They can also provide auction mechanisms, authentication, payment/settlement, and third-party logistics services. While payment/settlement and third-party logistics are already widely outsourced, other services (such as Open Ratings) that authenticate the credit and previous performance of buyers and sellers will increase in the future. Indeed, as third-party services proliferate, market makers can use them extensively to create hosted markets. (See "Hosted Markets.")

## HOSTED MARKETS

Hosted markets reflect a trend toward the use of specialists to custom-build electronic auctions. Consider, for example, how JC Penney implemented a dynamic pricing and auction solution to clear excess inventory via its Web site.

In 1999 the company wondered if it could bring its clearance merchandise to a wider audience, improve the speed at which merchandise moved, and increase the yield on what was sold, all at the same time. To do so, the company approached FairMarket, a provider of remote-hosted dynamic pricing and auction services. First, FairMarket and JC Penney developed an XML-based upload tool to streamline the process of uploading clearance items to FairMarket application servers.

Second, FairMarket provided a hosted service enabling two forms of transactions on JC Penney's clearance site: Automark-down, in which the price drops automatically over time if a product is not sold; and Auctions, in which buyers can bid on items. Third, FairMarket provided software to seamlessly integrate orders into JC Penney's fulfillment systems. Not only would goods be sold through JC Penney's own Web sites, but the FairMarket system (as a remote-hosted application) would permit customers to enter the JC Penney auctions from multiple sites (such as Yahoo.com).

Today's online markets are benefiting from the improvement in communications and computer technology. For instance, online markets are being assembled from various software components or hosted applications that are provided remotely over the Internet. These can create a seamless online marketplace. Like B2C transactions, B2B markets are similarly being constructed as best-of-breed applications and service providers and are electronically integrated into hosted markets.

The Envera Network, for instance, facilitates business among trading partners by providing a single point of contact for order fulfillment, financial settlement, monitoring, and tracking of

transactions. Envera has service alliances with First Union's
Commercial Banking Group, Miller Transporters (a tank truck carrier and third-party logistics company), and BDP International (a
global logistics and transportation company). In June 2001,
Envera, offering supply chain integration, combined forces with
ChemConnect, a marketplace for chemicals and plastics (see chapter 1). They formed—as they called it—a seamless connection,
from identifying new business partners to fulfillment. In this way,
hosted markets will continue to integrate diverse market functions
for the convenience of market makers, buyers, and sellers.

Another key risk market makers must address is technology failure. This is especially critical on the Internet, where
third parties control the quality of the communications infrastructure. Market reactions to technology failure can be
dire. When the eBay auction site crashed in June 1999, for
example, their stock slumped 21 percent in four hours.

Some technology risks can be managed through redundant systems. Others can be reduced by pretesting software.
Still other risks are not easily addressed. Each market maker
and market participant will have to decide how much technology risk he or she is willing to bear, and at what cost.

## Making Markets Work: A Framework for Action

How can managers systematically identify compelling opportunities for value creation? How can they find winning
strategies that drive to critical mass quickly and reduce transition risks?

We suggest the process/stakeholder benefit framework (see
table 3-1) that managers can use to systematically evaluate
market-making initiatives. This framework encourages managers not only to identify opportunities for new technologies

TABLE 3 - 1

## Process/Stakeholder Benefit Framework

| | NET BENEFITS TO STAKEHOLDERS | | |
|---|---|---|---|
| | Buyers | Market Makers | Sellers |
| **Processes** | | | |
| Search | | | |
| Pricing | | | |
| Logistics | | | |
| Payment and settlement | | | |
| Authentication | | | |
| Product representation | | | |
| Regulation | | | |
| Risk management | | | |
| Influence | | | |
| Dispute resolution | | | |
| Communications and computing (market platform) | | | |
| **Net Benefits** | **Positive or Negative?** | **Positive or Negative?** | **Positive or Negative?** |

For each process, conduct the five-step analysis:
1. Map the current structure of market processes.
2. Identify how new technologies may be used to reengineer major market processes.
3. Consider how required process changes will affect each stakeholder.
4. Develop strategies for attracting important stakeholders.
5. Develop an action plan for introducing the new trading processes.

among the different market processes (the vertical dimension of the framework), but also to determine the overall net benefits for each of the stakeholders (the horizontal dimension of the framework). By analyzing and designing different alternatives, one can determine the best alternative, that is, the one that creates the greatest sustainable value for all participants.

The process/stakeholder benefit framework has five steps. First, map how various trade processes are structured today for buyers and sellers. This provides the baseline for analysis.

Second, identify how new technologies may be utilized to reengineer major market processes. Managers must ask themselves the following types of questions:

- Search processes: What are the critical products and information that the buyers and sellers will search for? Should we use new search technologies or human brokers, or both (as in the case of Bandwidth.com)? Will the buyers want to buy from a set of prequalified suppliers, or from a broader pool of suppliers? How do we improve the search process for both buyers and sellers?

- Pricing processes: Will dynamic pricing add value for the buyers and sellers? What new pricing rules or auction mechanisms, enabled by technology, will efficiently match supply and demand? Do we need only one type of pricing mechanism, or several?

- Logistics processes: How can the transition from place to space reduce logistics, distribution, and handling costs? Can the digital representation of products and the decoupling of logistics and pricing processes for trading create substantial new value? Who benefits from the gains and who incurs new costs?

- Payment and settlement processes: What new payment and settlement systems will be enabled by new technologies? How do they create value for participants? How should they be integrated with other market processes?

- Authentication processes: How will electronic markets change the authentication processes? What new mechanisms must be put in place to help participants verify each other and the quality of goods and services? Who will bear the costs of new authentication processes?

In addition to these questions, managers must review the trade context processes that serve to enhance trust among the trading parties and legitimize the trade. These include:

- Product representation processes: How can new technologies change product representation? Will this adversely affect prices?

- Regulation processes: What rules of conduct are required to create trust in the electronic market? How will it fit in the legal framework that may cross various state and national boundaries?

- Risk management processes: What are the critical risks for sellers, buyers, and market makers? What new types of insurance or risk management systems are required to build trust in the market?

- Influence processes: How can market participants influence the behaviors of others to maintain trust in the market place? What feedback and ratings systems should be used to increase trust and persuade those who breach trust to improve their conduct?

- Dispute resolution processes: How will disputes be resolved in a decentralized electronic market? What forms of binding arbitration need to be created to build confidence in the market?

By asking these questions, managers can identify opportunities to create new value for market participants. 12Snap's founders, for instance, realized that new wireless systems allowed for an improved method of search and valuation. "Buying is something you do by yourself," says 12Snap cofounder Roeding. "But we realized that an auction is something you do with other people, and people want to have some entertainment—some fun."

By enabling market access to a greater variety of flowers, the Tele Flower Auction created compelling new value for growers and European buyers. But that value was boosted even further by putting the markets online and, therefore, decoupling logistics from search and valuation. Similarly, Aucnet dramatically reduced logistics requirements by keeping the car with the owner until it was sold, thus creating compelling value for both buyers and sellers.

The third step is to consider how the different stakeholders—the buyers, sellers, and market makers—will react to the required process changes. Do the process changes create benefits beyond those of the current model? Do the process costs go down (or up)? How do changes in any one process impact other processes? Are the net benefits of market innovations positive for all? As we learned from the Exmtrade example, this analysis of transition risks is critical.

Even if a new market is better than a traditional competitor, the demand for new skills or increases in costs—such as adding catalog information into a market—can prove fatal. In addition, changes in one process can impact another. In transitioning from place to space and using digital product representations, traditional authentication processes are disrupted. Both Aucnet and the TFA had to create new processes to reassure buyers. In the end both succeeded, and indeed Aucnet's model resulted in higher prices for sellers.

The fourth step is to develop strategies for getting the most important stakeholders to buy into the new market initiative. This may include inviting the largest buyers or sellers to be co-owners in order to drive instant liquidity into the new marketplace. By understanding the costs and benefits to buyers and sellers across the different processes, the market maker can selectively subsidize stakeholders to ensure their commitment to the market-making initiative.

## THE VALUE OF SOPHISTICATED MARKET PROCESSES

In order to better understand the Dutch flower markets, in the early 1990s we developed the process/stakeholder benefit framework.[8] More recently, Jochem Paarlberg at Erasmus University in Rotterdam adapted this framework to examine how the sophistication of any one process impacts market outcomes in terms of transaction volumes.[9]

This study examined 194 consumer Web auctions in eight European countries: Austria (8), Belgium (4), France (6), Germany (74), the Netherlands (40), Spain (5), Switzerland (27), and the United Kingdom (30). In each case each process was scored on a scale from 1 to 5 to define the maturity and sophistication of the process implementation (5 being the most "mature"). Each auction was also given an overall score from 1 to 5 based on individual process ratings.

The results of the classification of auctions showed that none had matured processes to the fullest extent. Twenty-three auctions had an overall maturity level of 4, 86 were at level 3, 82 were at level 2, and 3 auctions had a maturity level of 1. In analyzing the individual market processes, we found that the search, product representation, and legitimation processes were the most mature in the Web-based auctions.

When statistical analyses were undertaken, two additional results emerged. Higher levels of overall maturity were significantly related to the overall transaction volume of the auctions. Second, the top fifteen of the auctions in terms of transaction volumes were much better at executing the payment/settlement process and the influence processes than their peers.

Although we cannot establish a causal relationship between market process maturity and transaction volumes, this very preliminary study suggests that the level of process maturity is correlated to the success of the auction. It also outlines a potential application of the process/stakeholder benefit framework to assessing the maturity and capabilities of market-maker platforms.

The fifth step is to develop an action plan for introducing the new trading processes to buyers and sellers. Which processes will be transformed first; which can be deferred? New markets are not static; they are often a steppingstone in the evolution of trading. (Chapter 8 outlines some directions for market change.) In the transition from place to space, market makers must decide which features of the old market to retain, which processes to change, and when changes should be implemented.

The TFA, for example, carefully maintained the age-old Dutch auction mechanism for pricing because it was so familiar to both the buyers and sellers. This required considerable engineering effort since the bidders, who would be bidding simultaneously, were at multiple computers and locations. In time, TFA may introduce other pricing and transaction mechanisms, but in the beginning, familiarity has helped the new market work.

Creating and successfully implementing market innovations is not easy; markets touch a wide community of participants. To offer compelling value, critical mass, and reduced transition risks, it is vital for market innovators to have an in-depth understanding of trading processes, how they can be improved by new technologies, and their diverse impacts on all stakeholders. (See "The Value of Sophisticated Market Processes.") The process/stakeholder benefit framework is a tool to systematically explore these issues. With commitment and creativity, success can be yours.

# 4

## Auctions: The Devil
## Is in the Details

AS THE ECONOMY SLOWED in the summer of 2001, the electronics division of a diversified high technology company found its warehouse filling up with unsold computers, displays, and peripherals. Before long, inventory had grown from the customary one month to nearly two months. Worse still, a third of the inventory had become obsolete, due to the products' short life cycles.

To clear out the inventory, the company agreed to an auction strategy and hired a consulting firm to shape and execute the auction plan. To minimize the up-front costs to its client, the consulting firm created a value-based arrangement for their services, taking a percentage of the total sales transacted.

The consulting team first had to decide what kind of auctions they should hold. How much inventory should be released in each auction? What would the duration of each auction be? How could the auctions be conducted without undermining new product sales? Next, they had to settle on some of the finer details of the transactions. Should a reserve price or a minimum bid be set and, if so, how would it be determined? Should they charge a fixed shipping cost?

There were even more questions to be asked. How should they develop the auction catalog and customize it for specialized product configurations? What mix of products would attract the most bidders? How would they build the technology that would run several hundred of these auctions simultaneously—and in the end sell the 1,400 different kinds of items that were up for bid?

These were important questions. In fact, they illustrate a point made by economist Hal Varian: "Designing the right kind of auction will have as big an impact on the brand, customer loyalty, and profit margins of the undertaking as will the designing of the right kind of products."[1] In other words, while the choice of an auction is often straightforward, the path to success usually is not. Indeed, the devil is in the details.

Fortunately, the proliferation of Internet auctions has helped us understand these markets and their design better than ever before. Some firms are mastering these rules of market design and stand to profit handsomely by them. And so can you.

We believe there are three critical decisions involved in designing markets:

1. The selection of a revenue model for the market maker. This choice drives other market design choices.

2. The selection of an auction model—the rules by which bidding is conducted, information is revealed, and communications are structured between buyers, sellers, and market makers.

3. The selection of specific market features and strategies—for example, the way products are represented, the level of inventory provided, and the feedback offered buyers and suppliers.

## Selecting the Revenue Model

Electronic markets have four basic revenue models: fees per transaction, commissions on the value of transactions, subscription charges, and some combination of the above.

Fees per transaction is the most common model. Here, revenues are built from the transaction fees charged to the buyer, to the seller, or to both. There are several variations. One is a flat fee per transaction. Another, which is more common, is a percentage of the transaction price (this usually ranges between 1 percent and 10 percent). As the transaction volume (or transaction value) increases, the fee percentage for the transaction decreases. eBay, for example, charges buyers 5 percent of any amount under $25, 2.5 percent of any amount between $25 and $1,000, and 1.25 percent of any amount above $1,000 (as of December 2001).

Although transaction fees are popular, they are not perfect. One problem is that they charge only the customers who have made the successful bids, not those who have failed. Another problem is that they sometimes target the wrong end of the transaction. When there is a seller's market, for instance—in which there is more demand than supply—charging sellers is dunning the wrong side of the equation. The same rule applies, the other way around, in a buyer's market.

A third problem is that as transaction fees keep falling (in pace with new cost-cutting technologies or increased competition), the market institutions start losing revenues. In response, many are forced to create add-on fees. eBay, for example, charges service fees for featuring the item on its home page or other high visibility locations ($99.95); highlighting the auctioned product ($5.00); describing the product in bold ($2.00); or putting the product in the gallery ($0.25). Some markets bundle these services in flat membership or subscription fees, rather than charging customers per transaction. The revenue model that is chosen will depend to a great extent on the objectives of the market maker and the market participants. Some market makers offer a value-based arrangement, taking a commission on the total sales. This puts the market maker at risk, but ensures that the clients have low up-front costs and, in fact, could pay the auction or market fees from the proceeds of their sale.

An example of a subscription-based model is the Tyre Summits Trading Forum.[2] This marketplace, composed of tire and wheel suppliers around the world, charges $600 per year for membership and unlimited trading. As of late 2001, it had more than 2,500 members in 85 countries, with listings for $30 million worth of goods. This low-priced subscription fee model works only in markets with simple functionality— basic search and matching between buyers and sellers— where any particular buyer or seller trades infrequently.

## Selecting the Right Auction Model

What auction model will buyers, sellers, and market makers use in an electronic marketplace? Will it be unstructured— free-form negotiation—or structured, as in an auction with strictly prescribed rules for revealing buyer and seller preferences and price information?

### Dutch and English Auctions on the Internet

In almost every case (see "Major Auction Models"), the Internet has changed the form of auctions and given them greater possibilities. The main disadvantage of the English auction, for instance, was that it was not bounded in time. It was always a slow process, lasting hours or sometimes days. With the availability of remote bidding on the Internet, however, users no longer have to be in the auction room, thus reducing this drawback.

# MAJOR AUCTION MODELS

## The English Auction

The *English auction* is also called an ascending auction. It is used at Sotheby's, Christie's, and even eBay, and is most often associated with the selling of art, antiques, and other fine items. English auctions have been held since around 500 B.C. In the English auction, the auctioneer of a good or service begins with a reserve price and either increases the price in regular increments or lets bidders increase the price by whatever increments they want. In the ascending auction, the price is successively raised until only one bidder remains, and that bidder wins the object at the final price. As in the real world, the English auction is by far the most common type of auction on the Internet. In a randomly sampled survey of 200 Internet auctions, we found 85 percent to be variants of English auctions. Both Amazon and Yahoo!, for instance, use these variants.

## The Dutch Auction

The *Dutch auction* (or descending auction) was invented in the 1870s by a Dutch cauliflower grower, a farmer who wanted to simplify the selling of his product so he could concentrate on his crops. Unlike the more common English auction, where bidders push the price up from below, the Dutch method starts at a high price level set by the auctioneer—a level at which the good or service is very expensive and unlikely to be sold. The price then drops progressively, until a buyer signals to the auctioneer that he or she will take the goods at the current price. The auctioneer can announce the prices or may use an auction clock to indicate the current price.

The auction clock ticks downward until a buyer stops it by raising a hand, pushing a button, or by clicking the mouse of his computer. No actual sequential revelation of bids or preferences is involved. The bidder must choose how high to bid without knowing the other bidders' valuations or interests in the goods. As the announced price is progressively lowered, the buyer may get the goods at a lower price—but he could also lose them to another buyer, who may stop the clock first.

### First-Price and Second-Price Sealed-Bid Auctions

Auctions that utilize written bids are commonly referred to as *sealed-bid auctions.* Sequencing tends not to be a major issue in these auctions, since each bidder is normally allowed a single bid. Bidders in the first-price sealed-bid auction send in sealed bids to the auctioneer by a fixed time. The highest bidder (first price) wins the auction and gets the product or service. A bidder must decide how high to bid without knowing the bids of his competitors. In terms of the information revealed, first-price sealed-bid auctions are very similar to Dutch auctions.

The second-price sealed-bid or *Vickrey auction* was named after William Vickrey, Nobel laureate in economics, 1996. In this auction, the winner is the one with the highest bid, but he or she will pay only the second-highest price. Antebellum Covers uses this method to auction manuscripts and ephemera such as Civil War papers, small war relics, and eighteenth- and nineteenth-century war-related letters and documents.

In Antebellum's Vickrey auction, bids are accepted by mail, phone, or e-mail. Lots are sold to the highest bidder at one increment above the second-highest acceptable bid. For example, if the highest bid is $300 and the second-highest bid is $250, the high bidder pays only $260 ($250 plus the bidding increment of $10) instead of $300. All bids are confidential, and the high bid is not disclosed during the auction process. The elegance of the Vickrey auction is that it is designed in such a way that "truth telling"—bidding the true value of the auctioned product—is the best bidding strategy.

## The Double Auction

In a *double auction,* buyers and sellers each submit bids consisting of both a price and a desired quantity to an auctioneer. The auctioneer matches the sellers' offers (starting with the lowest price and then going up) to the buyers' offers (starting with the highest price and then going down) until all the quantities offered for sale are sold to the buyers. This type of auction works only for items that are traded in large quantities and are of known quality, such as securities or graded agricultural products. Double auctions can be operated in either sealed-bid or open-outcry formats.

The *sealed-bid double auction,* also called a clearinghouse auction, allows sellers to specify their offer prices, and buyers to specify their bids. The various offers and bids are matched in a fixed time using a simple algorithm. Each of the offers, with its price and volume, is mapped to create a supply curve. Next, each of the bids, with its price and volume, is mapped to create a demand curve. The clearinghouse price and volume traded are at the intersection of the two curves, as shown in figure 4-1. Buyers and sellers cannot modify their bids.

**FIGURE 4-1**

**Intersection of Supply and Demand Determines Clearinghouse Price**

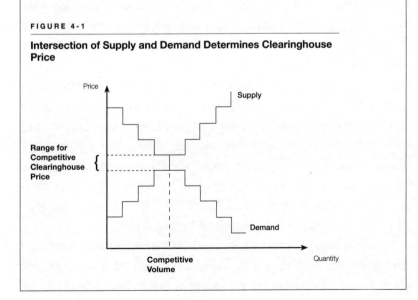

In a *call auction,* a variation of a double auction, trading takes place only at certain prearranged times—during the "calls." Between calls, orders accumulate. At the call, a price is established by identifying the supply and demand. Bringing sellers and buyers together at the same time, and at a single price, avoids the market spreads and random turbulence common in continuous markets.

In an *open-outcry double auction,* both offers and bids are updated continuously. Floor trading at the Chicago Commodities Exchange is one of the best-known examples of double auctions. Buyers and sellers are constantly revising their offers. The trades occur when the offer price and volume coincide with the bid price and volume. Open-outcry double auctions capture the preferences of sellers as well as buyers, allowing them to continuously adjust their offers and bids to adapt to varying market conditions and best match supply to demand.

The Dutch auction, meanwhile, has found great opportunities (and some particular problems) in entering the Internet age. A company called Intermodalex.com, for example, now provides a Dutch auction for shipping firms, which matches shipping services with customers who need to send products from the North Sea to ports around the world. To do this, the Intermodalex Web site lists and sells excess container space on oceangoing vessels. Since the excess container space is a perishable good, its value is effectively zero as soon as the ship casts off. It's also a commodity, since buyers know what a cargo hold looks like. In the end, the auction brings together the needs of both parties.

In this way, some Dutch markets have found success on the Internet. But they have also experienced problems. For one, Dutch auctions traditionally require the bidders to be located in the same place in order to make sure they can all respond at the same time. Unfortunately, since Internet traffic is often clogged, thereby delaying bids, a fast Dutch auction is difficult to run over the Internet today. Although this weakness has caused several Internet markets to fail, we expect the use of these auctions to grow as networks improve and new technologies guarantee that the most timely online bidders will win the auction.

While in theory the Dutch and English auction should lead to similar valuations of goods, in practice the Dutch method can generate higher prices for sellers. Why? Because in order to avoid losing a particular lot, buyers will often stop the clock at a higher price in a Dutch auction than they would bid in an English auction. Recognizing these advantages, a number of e-businesses are adopting the Dutch method.

Both English and Dutch auctions are used for "forward" auctions, but they can also be run as "reverse" auctions. In this case, the buyer is the bid-taker and the seller is the bidder. Most procurement auctions run in the reverse format. FreeMarkets, for example, employs English reverse auctions, using its Web-based software and hardware to permit businesses to solicit bids from suppliers. Thus, instead of the laborious process of sending out a request for proposal directly to many suppliers, a business can use FreeMarkets to do the work for them. Qualified suppliers can then submit offers through an auction. The supplier with the lowest bid wins, resulting in savings for the buyer. Best of all, FreeMarkets gives firms a way to get into electronic procurement without first investing in their own system.

### First-Price and Second-Price Sealed-Bid Auctions

The first-price, sealed-bid auction is also being adapted to the Internet. Century 21 Timeshare Resale International, for example, auctions off vacation timeshares to the highest bidder.

In practice, the second-price sealed-bid auction is seldom used, since once the highest price is discovered, the seller/auctioneer is rarely satisfied with the second-highest price. For that reason, bidders often worry that once their maximum bid is submitted, the auctioneer may unscrupulously act as if another bid were received—just under their maximum bid. Vickrey auctions work only when trust prevails among the sellers and buyers. For example, the majority of collectible stamp auctions, in which the traders trust one another and are seeking fair prices rather than exorbitant ones, use the Vickrey second-price rule.[3]

## The Double Auction

Internet double auctions work best when commodities are traded among large numbers of buyers and sellers. The U.S. utility ISO New England, for example, administers a "day-ahead/hourly" marketplace for wholesale electricity. In this auction, suppliers place bids for their available power resources the day before and submit separate bids for each resource for each hour of the day.

Next, ISO New England tabulates the bids and stacks them from lowest to highest, matching the expected hourly demand forecast for that hour and each hour in the next day. The power resources are then used to match the actual load, with the "market clearing price" for the power based on the highest-priced power resource used to meet that load. Market competition is driven by the fact that if a supplier bids too high a price for its power resources, then those resources aren't used, and the supplier receives no revenue. This encourages suppliers to bid the most competitive prices in order to earn revenue.

*Newer Auction Models*

With its combination of computational and communications power, the Internet enables market makers to shape more complex auction models than ever before. These include electronic Yankee auctions, multi-attribute auctions, and combinatorial auctions.

**Yankee Auctions** In a Yankee auction, identical items are offered simultaneously for sale. When the auction closes, the highest bidders win (at their bid price). More specifically:

- Bids are first ranked by price.

- If bid prices are the same, larger-quantity bids take precedence over smaller-quantity bids.

- If bid prices and quantities are the same, then earlier initial bids take precedence over later bids.

The Yankee auction is especially suited to selling large amounts of moderately priced items in small lot sizes.

**Multi-Attribute Auctions** Multi-attribute and combinatorial auctions are also recent arrivals that owe their existence to the availability of more powerful computers. In multi-attribute auctions, buyers searching and bidding for products specify the different prices they are willing to pay for products with various combinations of attributes. Likewise, sellers offer their products with multiple-attribute specifications.

With multi-attribute auction software one tries to find the best matches. For example, a buyer may be willing to buy 100 tons of a grade A chemical for $1,000 a ton, but is also willing to take 120 tons of a grade B of the same chemical at $600 a ton (and do some further refining of the product himself). With a multi-attribute auction, both the buyer and seller can find the best match among multiple alternatives.

In fact, Martin Bichler, associate professor at Vienna University of Economics and Business Administration, has shown that multi-attribute auctions do result in better outcomes for participants than single-attribute auctions.[4] More recently, Otto Koppius, assistant professor at the Rotterdam School of Management, elaborated on this finding in experiments on multi-attribute reverse auctions. In Koppius's studies, suppliers were bidding to provide a chemical product to a buyer. The chemical could vary in quality, delivery schedule, or offer-price in the auction. The auction was conducted in multiple rounds with four competing suppliers. At the end of each round the buyer would either indicate the rank order of preferences for different bidders' offers, or estimate how close (in terms of utility) the bidder was to the buyer's preferred configuration at that point in time.

The experiments showed that the greater the information feedback, the greater the chance for an optimal, efficient outcome.[5] The results also showed that the design of the information exchange is crucial when these auctions are executed over the Internet. Using multi-attribute auctions where suppliers or buyers can vary attribute levels creates potentially greater operational flexibility for both suppliers and buyers. Each can make new trade-offs in scheduling facilities and allocating resources based on different attribute level choices.

Multi-attribute auctions clearly have many advantages. But because most buyers and sellers do not yet understand the benefits of such dynamic pricing environments, they are as yet not widely used. Another reason for a reluctance to use these auctions is that in process industries, where the purity of, say, a chemical is vital, buyers generally prefer to contract with preferred suppliers—people who they believe can deliver the goods at the right time and with the highest quality. In the future, however, multi-attribute auctions may be used more frequently to price contracts with preferred suppliers. Perfect.com, for example, provides multi-attribute negotiation and auction software to various industries, from chemicals to seafood.

**Combinatorial Auctions**  Combinatorial auctions, in which combinations of items (rather than individual items) are traded, solve a different kind of resource allocation problem. Suppose an investor has a portfolio of stocks with a specific level of risk and wants to maintain that level of risk but shift his holdings to a different group of stocks. With a combinatorial auction, the investor could trade one portfolio for a portfolio held by someone else, without the expense of trading individual stocks.

Combinational bidding, meanwhile, is bidding with the goal of achieving higher value through the combination.[6] Bidders at the Federal Communications Commission's broadcast spectrum auctions, for example, may realize greater value for certain combinations of licenses, due to the synergies arising from owning licenses in adjoining geographic areas. In transport bidding, it may also be beneficial for a carrier to win bids on a group of continuous lanes. (A lane is a unique origin-destination pair requiring a specific type of service and equipment.)

Home Depot,[7] in fact, uses combinatorial bidding when contracting for carrier capacity.[8] Before the bidding begins, Home Depot provides potential bidders with origin and destination locations (e.g., retail stores, supplier locations, or distribution centers), lane details, and demand forecasts. Lanes can be point-to-point (e.g., vendor to distribution center), point-to-zone (e.g., distribution center to cluster of stores), zone-to-point (e.g., cluster of vendors to distribution center), or zone-to-zone (e.g., cluster of vendors to cluster of stores). For each lane, Home Depot specifies the origin and destination, average route distance, average number of stops, demand forecast, equipment requirements, and service requirements.

Given this information, the carriers prepare their bids, which may include combinations of lanes as well as individual lanes. The carriers may also specify constraints on available capacity (e.g., the maximum amount of business awarded in a geographic area) or submit conditional bids (e.g., a carrier may submit two combinations and request that only one of the two be awarded). Home Depot can also impose restrictions on winning bids. For instance, it could restrict the number of carriers that are awarded freight across the entire network. After collecting the bids, Home Depot uses integer programming to select a subset of these bids that best satisfies its needs. Although Home Depot currently uses these bids for full truckload shipments, it is expanding this bidding to smaller shipments as well.

## Emerging Auctions Meet Specialized Needs

The auction examples in this section illustrate the increasing variety of auction methods and the greater specialization of auctions to customer needs. They also illustrate another important value added by electronic auctions: Auctions allow buyers and sellers to buy, sell, or reconfigure goods into new bundles with different "risk-effort-reward" possibilities than they might have been able to achieve through other sales or purchase channels.

German air carrier Lufthansa, for instance, uses the English auction mechanism to rid itself of excess seat inventory. Lufthansa holds fifty auctions monthly, one for each set of tickets to a certain destination. The auctions are held between 10 A.M. and 10 P.M. and draw an average of sixty participants per auction. Lufthansa implemented this auction to attract potential customers without incurring massive advertising costs or alienating traditional distribution partners. The tickets are carefully selected to avoid empty seats in specific routes. Lufthansa also obtains customer feedback, researches preferences in the market, and gets plenty of publicity in the traditional media.

Emerging types of auctions, then, give suppliers new ways of managing inventory and demand risk. They also help segment customers based on their price and risk sensitivity. Customers, meanwhile, are afforded new kinds of "risk-reward" preferences. For example, if a traveler needed to go from one city to another for an important meeting, he would probably want a guaranteed seat, and he would be willing to pay full fare for it. But if his schedule were flexible and he wanted the cheapest seat possible, he might choose an auction where he could bid for an inexpensive ticket.

We expect that online auctions will become increasingly popular as traders, businesses, and consumers become more familiar with them. In the next section, therefore, we will focus on designing these new markets and auctions in greater detail. We also examine the total costs of transactions, of which auctions are still a small part. Ultimately, auctions form a part of a broader set of activities necessary to trade goods or services. These related activities and the context of the trade are likely to affect the feasibility of specific auctions in different markets. As illustrated by FreeMarkets, Intermodalex, and Home Depot, we expect auction models to become increasingly specialized in the years ahead.

## Managing the Details

To create a successful and cost-efficient market, there are several factors to take into account:

- The number of competing bidders and bids
- Whether the offerings should be single- or multiple-unit

- The sequence of offerings
- The auction inventory
- The product description and product representation method
- The duration and time of the auction (including the ending day)
- The speed of the auction
- The buyer, seller, and product rating mechanisms
- The minimum bid and reserve price level
- The fixed-price components in the total auction price
- The feedback to bidder

## The Number of Bidders and Bids

The number of bidders participating in an auction determines the level of competition among them. As a number of studies have shown, the higher the number of bidders, the more intense the competition, and the higher the selling price.[9] Thus, auctioneers whose revenue models depend on the selling price (such as those who earn commissions on the value of the transactions) should actively seek to increase the number of qualified participants.

Emerging Internet technologies, combined with direct mail and other marketing techniques, allow auctioneers to inexpensively invite bidders to participate in online auctions. WayBid.com, for example, provides technologies to link multiple electronic marketplaces together in real time, increasing the number of both buyers and sellers and thus improving liquidity. Proxy bidding, in which a software program bids for you during the auction, can also encourage bidder participation. Because it frees them from having to constantly monitor an auction, a proxy bidding system can attract participants who would otherwise be too busy to take part.

Multiple auction services and proxy bidding systems can directly increase the revenues and profits of both the auctioneer and seller. But even those who make their money with subscription charges or transaction fees should have some incentive to use them, since both sellers (who will see more buyers) and buyers (who will have more product alternatives) will be drawn to the site with the greatest number of participants, and thus more liquidity.

### Single versus Multiple Units

Although auctions have been typically used for single-unit products, multi-unit auctions have recently been attracting increasing attention. There are two different pricing rules used in multi-unit, ascending-bid auctions. First, there is the discriminatory or pay-your-bid rule, where each winning bidder pays the amount of their own bid.

For example, we have seen Egghead use a discriminatory, multi-unit, ascending-price auction, or, as they call it, a Yankee auction. When forty new digital cameras are auctioned in the Yankee auction, the winners pay a price depending on their final bids. In this case, it is possible that the number one bidder pays $350 for the camera and number forty pays $280—for the very same camera.

Second is the uniform-price rule, in which each winning bidder pays the amount of the lowest accepted bid. eBay holds these uniform-price, multi-unit, ascending-price auctions.[10] Suppose a seller on eBay has ten pens that he prices for sale at a dollar each. If there are ten participants who bid a dollar for one pen, then each of those participants will have bought a pen for a dollar. If, on the other hand, there are five participants who bid $1.25 for one pen, and ten participants who bid a dollar for a pen, then each of the $1.25 bidders and the five earliest $1.00 bidders will get a pen. However, both the $1.25 bidders and the $1.00 bidders will pay only a dollar, since all the winning bidders must pay the same price—which is the lowest successful bid.

It may sound complicated, but most of these auctions end simply: Most participants win the items they bid on at the minimum asking price. However, there are some special, less intuitive possibilities. The lowest bidder, for instance, may specify a multiple quantity and not receive that full quantity. Why? Because after the higher bidders get their share, there may not be enough left over. In other words, if the lowest bidder requests a quantity of three pens, but nine pens have already gone to the higher bidders, she will get only the one remaining pen. The only way to prevent this is not to be the lowest bidder.

Will uniform or discriminatory price auctions lead to higher prices for the seller? When should one model be chosen over the other? The answers are yet to be determined.

## The Sequence of Offerings

In the traditional English and Dutch auctions, the sequence of the offerings is important. Fish peddlers, for example, want to see all their fish auctioned off as early as possible, knowing that the price will drop as the day progresses. (This is known as the "declining price anomaly.") But whose products should be auctioned first? To keep things fair, auctions hold lotteries to determine the order of offerings during the auction. Thus each seller has a chance to go first. This rule is just as important in Internet auctions. The Pan European Fish Auctions, for example, use such lotteries.

## The Auction Inventory

Sellers and auctioneers can also work product inventory to their advantage. As inventory declines, after all, prices may rise. The auctioneer and seller must decide on the amount of inventory to be released, based on the trade-off between the costs of holding inventory and the losses when excess inventory discounts prices.

How can companies strategically determine the amount of inventory to release? One way is to release a large amount of inventory on the first day of a new product introduction, observing how much buyers are willing to pay for it. In multi-unit auctions, there will typically be a spread in the prices paid by the buyers. By looking for break points in the spread and analyzing the pattern of demand represented by the final prices, the auctioneer can decide how much inventory to release the next day.

Consider an Egghead auction for an Agfa scanner (described in more detail in chapter 7). Fifteen units were put up for sale, with thirteen bids received, ranging from $21 to $45. Since the highest two prices were nearly double the lowest price (and nearly 50 percent greater than the median price), the auctioneer could release just two units instead of fifteen the next time around. Using auctions to determine the demand curve and strategically releasing future inventory, then, is one way to increase the auction price. If the auctioneer's objective were to maximize transactions, on the other hand, it would have been better to increase the inventory, waiting until the price dropped to the point that discouraged sellers.

## Product Representation

The fact that bidders cannot see the product up close is the biggest difference between auctions held a decade ago and

those facilitated by the Internet today. As a result, auctioneers are trying to replace intimacy with enough digital information to encourage people to participate. Is a picture worth
a thousand words? How does product representation impact
the final auction price? In general, photographs are especially valuable in conveying information about unique
goods. But how do they compare with the real thing?

It is not clear to what extent proximity affects the final
auction price, and researchers are looking for answers. The
"Impact of eAuctions" Research Program at Erasmus University in Rotterdam has several studies underway to analyze
the impact of product representation. As yet the results are
inconclusive. In one study of Beanie Baby collectibles on
Yahoo! auctions, offering a digital picture had no significant
impact on the final auction price. In contrast, placing a digital picture of the PalmPilot on eBay had a definite positive
impact on its final auction price. Perhaps bidders require
more information only while considering a higher-cost good
(such as a PalmPilot). Or perhaps Beanie Baby collectors already know the product. In another study of eBay auctions,
Professors Charles Wood and Robert Kauffman found that a
picture of coins raised the average price by almost 12%.[11]

Other descriptions do affect the sale, however. For example, eBay provides sellers with both a short title, to grab a
buyer's attention, and a longer description activated by clicking on the short title. eBay also allows sellers to put the title
and descriptions in boldface or to attach a gift icon. The gift
icon, which costs the seller $1, highlights items that might
make good gifts. Items with the icon are also listed in a special gift section. Similarly, an icon adjoining the item title
alerts bidders when a digital photograph is available. eBay
also places a "hot" icon next to any item that receives thirty-
one or more bids, signaling substantial buyer interest.

Whether these descriptive techniques affect the final price
and the number of bidders and bids is still under study.

However, some early results suggest that rich textual descriptions of "experience" goods, such as wine or clothing, can compensate to some degree for the inability of buyers to taste, touch, and see them up close. Other research suggests that moving from real life to digital imagery changes the way bidders value the product, and hence the overall auction price.

A study of the Dutch flower auctions, however, is revealing.[12] When bidders were shown digital photographs of Anthuriums, rather than the real flowers, the average final bid dropped 6.5 cents per flower, or by roughly 5 percent of the average price. One explanation might be that digital images do not convey the assurance of flower quality that real flowers do. The drop in the bid price may reflect, therefore, the bidders' uncertainties and risk. Another explanation is that bidders in electronic auctions may focus more on other, more objective, quantitative data of the flower lot, because that is the only data they have. Therefore, characteristics like stem length and diameter have a stronger effect on the price level than in traditional auctioning.

## Auction Duration and Time of Auctions

The length of the auction is another consideration. Sellers on eBay, for example, can decide between three-, five-, seven-, and ten-day auctions. (All eBay auctions are English auctions, with a fixed end time and date.) But do longer auctions on the Internet pay off? In general, longer English auctions on the Internet tend to attract more bidders and earn higher prices. For other auction types this relationship is not as discernible.

Dutch auctions are typically much shorter. For example, Dutch auctions at Wehkamp, a catalog retailer, are over in a couple of minutes. Auction rounds done in the Dutch style at the Dutch flower auctions take an average of four seconds.

Dutch auctions, then, match supply and demand very quickly. The shorter the duration, the more transactions the auctioneer can complete. The time at which auctions are conducted is also an increasingly important variable. Consumers visit auctions more often during the weekend, and weekend auction revenues seem to be higher than those held during the week. Thus, business-to-consumer sellers are advised to schedule the close of their auctions on the weekend. B2B auctions, in contrast, should be conducted during the week. This was as true fifty years ago as it is today, and the Internet has not changed that rule.

## Auction Speed

In addition to the time and duration of an auction, the speed at which an auction is held can affect prices. In English auctions, the speed of the auction is determined by the starting point and the fixed ending or, when there is no announced end to the bidding, by the lack of subsequent bids. Experienced auctioneers, of course, can affect the tempo of bidding, raising the bid levels quickly or slowly to encourage competition.

In contrast to the English auctions, Dutch auctions rely on the price interval of each clock "tick" and the speed of the clock itself to set the tempo of the auction. In a Dutch flower auction, for example, one clock tick represents one cent, five cents, ten cents, or even one hundred cents. The speed of the clock varies between one tenth of a second and a full second per tick (the average transaction time is four seconds). How fast the clock advances from one tick to the next determines how quickly the price will fall.

A preliminary study of Dutch auction speeds found that high-priced clock ticks (a dollar versus fifty cents) or higher clock speeds tended to lower the average auction price. The combined effect of a high clock tick and high clock speed, meanwhile, significantly dropped prices, benefiting the buyers. The effect of auction speed in English auctions is the opposite—higher auction speed caused higher auction prices.

The difference between the effects of auction speed on English versus Dutch auctions suggests the need to select the speed of the auction process carefully in order to optimize prices.[13] On one hand, computerization makes it easier to control the speed of auctions. On the other hand, fast auctions over the distributed Internet are difficult to implement, since traffic snarls can prevent the timely delivery of bids. We expect the use of fast electronic auctions to grow, particularly as networks improve and new technologies can guarantee that the timeliest online bidder will actually win the auction.

## Buyer, Seller, and Product Ratings

A key innovation behind the success of eBay was the introduction of a simple feedback-rating system, one that encouraged trust between buyers and sellers. With this system, eBay allows buyers and sellers to rate their experiences with each other in order to promote confidence among participants. Buyers and sellers have the opportunity to rate each other as positive (+1), neutral (0), or negative (-1). Any time a trader is identified on the site, his cumulative feedback rating number is displayed in parentheses.

Traders with ratings higher than 10 receive a "star," a graphic icon whose color changes to indicate larger and larger rating numbers. Anyone whose rating goes below –4 is prohibited from using the site any further. Traders can also view the feedback comments left by other traders about any individual. Typical examples of positive comments are:

"Very reliable seller, received products within a week."

"Excellent buyer, paid promptly."

Typical negative comments are:

> "I sent money promptly. However, after two months I have not received the items."

> "Items did not come with the promised extras."

A study that examined feedback ratings discovered that users of eBay primarily focus on negative rating points.[14] Whenever negative feedback appeared, it caused a substantial decrease in auction price. Increases in positive ratings, on the other hand, had minimal effect. This suggests that buyers tend to focus disproportionately on trading risks, are risk-averse, and discount prices as a risk premium when dealing with traders with a low rating or bad reputation. It also suggests that if an auction house is dependent on commissions for revenue, then it should take steps to protect its customers and reputation by encouraging and monitoring feedback, and periodically expunging vendors and buyers with consistently bad reputations. The auction house can also work to help errant suppliers and buyers restore their ratings after a probationary period to help their reputations improve.

### The Minimum Bid and Reserve Price Levels

Auctioneers and sellers can vary a number of features related to price. For example, they can set a minimum bid level, which puts a floor beneath the subsequent bidding. Sellers like minimum bids because they mitigate their risk. On the other hand, a minimum price, especially a high minimum price, can discourage potential bidders. What research is available suggests that minimum bid levels do not significantly affect final selling prices.

Sellers may also set a reserve price level, which is a kind of undisclosed minimum bid. Bidders will usually be informed that there is a reserve price, but will not be told exactly what that price is. Unless a bid exceeds the set reserved price, the seller will refuse to complete the transaction. Neither reserve prices nor minimum bids guarantee the seller that he will get the price he wants, but they do ensure that he will not have to sell at a price he cannot afford. The presence of a reserve price can have the same discouraging effect on potential bidders as a minimum price. It reduces the probability that the winning bid will actually result in a transaction. Empirical research suggests that reserve prices act as additional bidders, at least until the reserve price is met, and thus tend to drive up the final auction price.

### Fixed Fees

Auctioneers and sellers can also add a fixed fee to the final auction price—for example, a shipping charge or transaction fee. Research in consumer behavior shows that partitioning the price into multiple components often increases demand and reduces the buyer's ability to recall the total price. In a recent study of eBay, Professors Gerald Hauble and Peter Popowski Leszczyc of the University of Alberta found that the total selling prices were higher when there was a fixed-price shipping charge as compared to no shipping charge.[15] They also found that the harder it is to value the good for sale, the higher the positive impact of a fixed price on the total sale. It would seem, then, that consumers in real-world online auctions are failing to properly account for fixed-price components, which should give sellers the opportunity to systematically manipulate auctions in their favor.

### Feedback to the Bidder

Auctioneers can also vary the feedback provided to bidders. This feedback may, for example, include the current high bid, or all the bids by all bidders. In general, Dutch auctions do not provide any feedback, except for the name of the winner and the winning price. Nor do single-round, sealed-bid auctions provide feedback. However, in a multiple-round, sealed-bid auction or in an English auction, information feedback can be given on bids, bid scores, bid rankings, utility functions, and bidder identities. Recent literature and experiments suggest that the more information provided to bidders, the quicker the auction converges to a final price—and, the data suggests, to a higher price. Information on other bidders and their bids seems to have the most impact. So, the Internet allows us to implement multiple-round auctions more easily, and therefore information feedback becomes a more critical component in the auction design.

### Putting It All Together

At the beginning of this chapter we presented the case of a high-tech manufacturer burdened with excess inventory. Here's how their consulting team solved the problem. They first had to choose the auction model. They could have chosen a Dutch auction model for liquidating inventory quickly, but it was not clear that this would generate the best price. Since the team wanted to maximize the value to the client (and themselves), and because the technology allowed them to conduct many auctions simultaneously, they chose a modified English auction approach that would run for multiple days. The longer duration allowed more bidders to participate and compete, in contrast to a descending-price Dutch auction that requires simultaneous participation by all bidders for a short period of time.

The team also decided on the finer details. They decided to set a reserve price at or above half the expected price for the item. Reserve prices for newer items were set closer to the prices normally offered by the sales force. No shipping or handling prices were added, as the client absorbed them.

Meanwhile, the team supervised the production of a cata-log from available spec sheets, with provisions to add sec-tions that would be customized for specialized configura-tions. The catalog was put together before the auctions started, although the inventory that would be sold in each auction had not yet been fully determined. This would give the salespeople additional time to make the sale through the normal sales channel.

To find bidders, the team first divided the possible cus-tomers into eighteen different categories. Working with the sales team, they recognized that each segment would be in-terested in a different subgroup of the inventory. This would allow simultaneous or overlapping auctions offering a prod-uct mix of interest to a specific segment. To get enough bid-ders, the team worked with the client's sales force to alert po-tential buyers in the distributor, retail, wholesale, and corporate buyer categories, using communications tools from the phone to faxes. To avoid channel conflict and to get buy-in from the sales force, the team convinced the division vice president to agree that the sales force would get commis-sions on any auction-based sales to their specific customers.

As for the technology, the team chose Moai auction soft-ware that would allow many hundreds of users to participate. Running the auctions over a one-month time frame, the team successfully cleared much of the client's inventory. This was especially useful for the outdated equipment, and the client learned the auctions could provide an entirely new channel to customers. When the equipment was newer and minimum prices were higher, the auctions were less effective.

## Bedeviled by Costly Details

Not paying attention to the details can be very costly. Consider the Universal Mobile Telecommunications System (UMTS) auction in the Netherlands. It started July 6, 2000, with five lots (two high-bandwidth licenses and three lower-bandwidth licenses). The bid-taker and designer of the auction was the Dutch government (who designed the auction with the counsel of some Ph.D. game theorists). Six companies were qualified as bidders. The results of every bidding round were published on the Internet.

The auction was structured as a multiple-round, sealed-bid auction that allowed users to use the "pass" sealed bid. In this case, bidders could choose to pass on offering a bid three times during the first thirty rounds without exiting the auction. Normally participants can use "pass" bids only at the end of the auction in order to temporarily exit the auction and revise strategy or arrange new financing. Moreover, another rule stipulated that if all the bidders used the "pass" sealed bid, then the bid-taker, the Dutch government, had to discount the price level by 30 percent. The participants took advantage of these two rules, using the "pass" bids in the first three rounds and forcing the government to lower the prices from an initial 100 million Dutch guilders toward zero guilders. Poor auction design proved to be a costly mistake.

Auction markets must be designed to be robust in extreme situations. Consider the electricity crisis in California. Prices in California's competitive wholesale electricity market increased by 500 percent between the second half of 1999 and the second half of 2000.[16] While wholesale prices rose dramatically, retail prices were capped until early in 2001. As a result, California's two largest utilities were paying far more for wholesale power than they were able to resell it for at retail. Both became insolvent in January 2001 and one declared bankruptcy in April 2001. As utilities' credit problems became evident, suppliers began to stop selling power to them, causing rolling blackouts in California. The state of California stepped in and used state funds to buy power from unregulated wholesale suppliers to avoid widespread blackouts, spending about $8 billion between January and May

2001. It also negotiated long-term contracts (up to twenty years) with suppliers via an Internet-based auction.

This result was certainly not planned when the California electricity market was restructured in 1996. The rationale behind the reform was that wholesale prices would be lower than the regulated retail price of generation service.[17] Central to the reform was the setup of two institutions: the California Independent System Operator (ISO) and the California Power Exchange (PX). The ISO was responsible for operating the transmission networks. The PX ran day-ahead and hour-ahead hourly public wholesale auctions for sales of energy. The utilities had to place their day-ahead demand through the PX on an hourly basis. They also had to bid all of the energy supplied from any generating units they owned. Other generators and other demand-serving organizations could voluntarily trade in the PX. The PX took the hourly day-ahead supply and demand bids and aggregated them to form aggregate supply and demand curves for each hour. The hourly market clearing price was determined by the intersection of these curves. All buyers paid and all sellers received this uniform market clearing price.

During low- and moderate-demand conditions, the markets appeared to be quite competitive, with day-ahead prices reasonably close to estimates of marginal cost. But during high-demand conditions, it became clear that the market was clearing at prices far above the marginal cost of the most expensive generators. Generators began to realize that a small amount of capacity withholding could lead to large price increases.

Paul Joskow, a Massachusetts Institute of Technology professor of economics and management, showed that the combination of inelastic demand and tight supplies in the California electricity market created opportunities for individual suppliers to exercise market power without engaging in collusion, driving prices up still higher. Joskow and his colleagues found that about a third of the wholesale prices could be attributed to market power after accounting for changes in fundamental supply and demand conditions.

The utilities announced that they had ceased payments, and as a result the PX stopped operating its day-ahead markets on January 31, 2001. California had not taken into account that auction markets in extreme situations—such as high-demand conditions—need to be carefully tested and evaluated.

The moral of this story is that auction designs need to be tested through simulations before they are introduced in order to prevent the suboptimal outcomes that occurred in the Dutch UMTS auction or the extreme outcomes of the California Power Exchange. Smart bidders will exploit poor auction design, even if they do not explicitly collude. This makes careful auction selection and design increasingly important.

## A Thoughtful Approach

Given the plethora of design choices, you might feel you need a Ph.D. or two to effectively design new electronic markets. Sometimes you do. But as the Dutch UMTS and California Power Exchange auctions show, even the "experts" can get it wrong.

Good market and auction design is not easy. However, we believe a disciplined approach to selecting the revenue models and the auction model and systematically considering the different design elements can greatly enhance the probabilities of success. We also suggest that firms take a flexible, iterative design-and-build strategy. As it is difficult to predict the impact of different variables and the cross-relations between variables, market makers should systematically experiment to identify which variables will most affect the price, volume, or other desired outcomes in the context of their industry or application. By testing different designs across different products or customer segments, they can discover the best strategies for maximizing profit. In doing this, they should vary auction designs in the least disruptive way to customers. If live experiments are infeasible, simulations may be helpful in testing the model and improving it. Those who evolve better designs will realize better returns.

The science of how to best design electronic markets and auctions is still evolving. What we have presented here is only a snapshot of current practices. But market and auction applications always fall within the context of broader business objectives. Understanding the broader business context is critical in order to avoid channel conflicts, get content online effectively, and attract organizational buy-in. Thus, the most effective and profitable approaches to implementing markets will combine heuristics and sound business judgment along with knowledge of the science of auctions and market design.

# 5

---

# Using B2B Markets in the
# Supply Chain

VERTICALNET WAS ONCE a high flyer in the B2B business, creating and operating more than sixty different electronic markets in different industries. But when the dot-coms collapsed, so did VerticalNet, its market value plunging sharply to $100 million from $15 billion only two years earlier. Today VerticalNet is out of electronic markets almost entirely, and instead is playing the role of an enterprise software company, one that helps its customers set up private marketplaces and better integrate their supply chains.

VerticalNet is not the only market maker trying to remake itself. Ventro, which operated the Chemdex marketplace, now offers software collaboration tools for supply chains as well as other consulting services. SciQuest, which operated specialized exchanges for laboratory scientists to access specialty chemicals, now provides research asset management tools and services. ChemConnect, which still operates the World Chemical Exchange, also helps customers track orders and manage logistics online and enables suppliers to connect to the private exchanges of companies. As these firms and many others have discovered, it's difficult to make money in B2B.

Despite the well-publicized B2B market failures, we believe auctions and electronic markets will be a permanent fixture in the business landscape. In this chapter[1] we examine the changing role of auctions and electronic markets in the supply chain and address three key questions:

- How can companies use auctions and B2B markets to realize value in the supply chain?

- What are the different types of B2B markets, and how should companies choose to participate in them?

- What are the integration challenges companies must overcome to fully realize the value of B2B markets and exchanges?

## Electronic Sourcing through Reverse Auctions

Reverse auctions, in which a single buyer puts out a request for a quote and multiple sellers bid until the lowest offer-price is discovered, are proving to be one of the most useful applications of B2B. Auctions have many potential applications in the supply chain, from liquidating excess inventory, as discussed in the last chapter, to discovering prices and sourcing key materials. Typically, these auctions run for an hour or two, with three to ten competing bidders.

Reverse auctions are used not just for commodities, but for sourcing a wide range of products, from specialized telecommunications equipment to temporary manpower services. Today the savings from these electronic auctions are fueling their rapid proliferation as a way of transacting business. Because the savings average 19 percent—and sometimes reach 50 percent[2]—and because reverse auctions can slash procurement times dramatically, they are increasingly popular.

Consider the case of a global airline and its purchase of personal computer consumables, such as paper, printer cartridges, or floppy disks. As figure 5-1 shows, the airline held a

**FIGURE 5-1**

## Global Airline's One-Hour Reverse Auction for PC Consumables

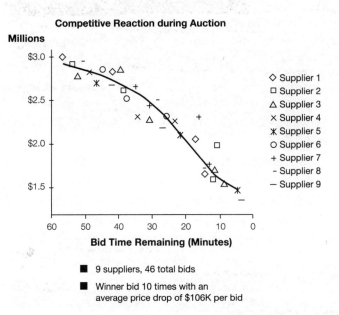

**Competitive Reaction during Auction**

◇ Supplier 1
□ Supplier 2
△ Supplier 3
× Supplier 4
✻ Supplier 5
○ Supplier 6
+ Supplier 7
- Supplier 8
— Supplier 9

- 9 suppliers, 46 total bids
- Winner bid 10 times with an average price drop of $106K per bid

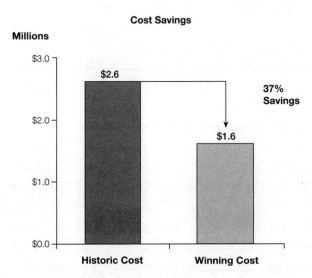

**Cost Savings**

*Source:* © 2001 Accenture. Used with permission.

one-hour auction with nine bidders and was able to save $1 million—37 percent below its normal costs.

But reverse auctions deliver more than savings. They also help buyers gain useful information, ultimately revealing the supplier's bottom line or reserve price. The auction process is also more efficient than traditional negotiation processes. It reduces the skill levels and time required for negotiation; shortens time frames, thus forcing quicker decisions from suppliers; and provides a more objective basis for deciding contract awards.

Given the advantages that reverse auctions offer the buyers, one might wonder what's in it for the sellers. A great amount, it turns out: Sellers realize the reverse auction is a more open bidding process, with motivated and committed buyers. Auctions enable sellers to better understand competitor pricing, compress the time frame to make a sale, and reduce the handling costs of tenders. Furthermore, sellers benefit from shorter sales cycles and faster contract awards, enabling better planning. Besides, sellers realize that while prices may fall in one auction, they may subsequently rise in another, depending on demand and supply.

But to really seize the value of reverse auctions, companies need to do more than simply hire an auction service. Rather, the true value of reverse auctions is realized when companies engage in a broad and efficient strategic sourcing process, one in which auctions are but one step in the overall plan. Companies have different levels of sourcing expertise and capabilities. Some companies have critically analyzed their categories of spending, identified savings opportunities, and prequalified and rationalized the supplier base; they understand the likely total cost of ownership of the product or service being purchased. Companies that are less advanced in their sourcing capabilities should start with this type of research. Part of this preauction analysis should include an assessment of the total cost of product ownership. (Value is not just realized in cheaper purchase costs, after all, but in savings in the total cost of ownership.)

Based on this analysis, buyers should next develop their product requirements and materials specifications and identify likely suppliers. In general, a small number of suppliers (less than ten) is best, so that each has a good chance of winning the contract. This encourages them to put the time and money into the information and specifications package the tender requires.

Next, suppliers unfamiliar with auctions need to be trained in the bidding process. Suppliers generally learn quickly how to bid (see chapter 7), but occasionally some suppliers bid too aggressively, making bids that fall below their costs just to win a contract. If not managed properly, such underbidding can put both the supplier and buyer at risk—especially if the supplier's business fails as a consequence.

David Nelson, vice president for worldwide supply management at Deere & Company and a recognized innovator in sourcing and procurement, explains how his company once addressed the issue. Deere was running a reverse auction, and at one point a longtime supplier underbid precariously in order to maintain the company as a customer. Fortunately, the Deere procurement team recognized the scale of the risk to the supplier and quickly dispatched a team of engineers to help the supplier deliver on the bid price without going broke. Although such situations rarely work out so well for either party, thanks to Deere's partnering mind-set, both companies won.

Generally, we have found that auctions with the most flexible rules are the most satisfactory. For instance, one auction rule states that the auction ends when no bidder has lowered the price in the last five minutes. This rule does not mandate, however, that the next bid must be lower than the current lowest bid—only that a bidder must lower his bid

below his previous bid within five minutes to keep the auction going. Sometimes the auction process is viewed primarily as a price-discovery mechanism, and the buyer does not
have to choose the lowest bidder. While this is frowned upon
by suppliers, it allows the buyer to select a supplier who may
be a strategic choice for reasons other than price. Today,
companies are using reverse auctions for purchasing both direct and indirect materials and services. From rivets to manpower services, companies are finding tremendous savings
and new efficiencies. Electronic reverse auctions not only
generate savings from price competition, but in combination
with a disciplined sourcing process, can also cut the procurement time from about five months to less than six weeks.

We believe that auctions are most effective when they are
part of a broader strategic sourcing process. As the Deere &
Company example illustrated, buyers and sellers must balance their short- and long-term needs wisely. Buyers must
ensure that they not only get a good price, but also obtain
good service and supplier's investments in innovations that
will meet future buyer needs. Thus, prequalifying suppliers
and developing a stable supplier base for specialized materials is critical for long-term success. Given the preauction
preparation required and the need to ensure that the auction
choice is strategically aligned with the firm's longer-term
sourcing objectives, we find that this method is most suitable
for transactions in excess of $250,000.

## B2B Electronic Markets: Independent, Consortia, and Private Exchanges

A few years ago, everyone seemed to be creating an electronic
market. Companies on the bandwagon included software providers like Ariba, Commerce One, and SAP; content
providers such as VerticalNet; and even traditional compa-

nies like Ford, General Motors, and Chrysler. In the beginning of 2000, some industry analysts even predicted that 10,000 electronic markets would flourish by 2004. Many of the electronic markets were established on the premise of "If you build it, they will come." But by the second quarter of 2000, it was clear that they would not come, and the same analysts that praised the electronic market boom were now speaking of a shakeout that would eliminate all but a few markets in each industry.

In reality, three kinds of B2B exchanges have emerged over the years: the independent exchange, the consortium exchange, and the private exchange. Independent exchanges are electronic markets established by third parties that link buyers and sellers. Examples include Chemdex, PaperX, PEFA, and PartMiner. Consortia exchanges, or industry-sponsored markets, are set up jointly by a group of key players, either buyers or sellers. Key examples are Covisint in automotive, Exostar in aerospace, Quadrem in metals and mining, and Pantellos in the electric utilities industry. Private exchanges, on the other hand, are trading platforms set up by individual companies to directly reach their key suppliers or customers. Examples include Cisco and Dell's private exchanges with key suppliers and customers.

These three B2B models were created with the radical promise of dramatically reducing procurement costs. They promised to leverage the Internet as a communications platform, providing buyers and sellers with more information on each other's needs as well as the available products for sale. They also promised to generate more competition among suppliers, enable consolidation of purchases across multiple buyers, and improve coordination between buyers and sellers. Despite many failures of each type of exchange, each model has a place in the supply chains of different industries.

## Independent Exchanges

Early in the development of B2B electronic markets, a number of independent exchanges were created, backed by venture capitalists and promoted by industry analysts. Many of these exchanges promised benefits that included expanded access to a larger supplier or buyer base, a single virtual venue for conducting business, the efficient management of business relationships, and expanded visibility into prices around the world. However, many of them misjudged how much customers were willing to pay for their services, the changes required of customers, and the costs of acquiring customers. Furthermore, many of the businesses started without the buy-in of key buyers and suppliers. In addition, many of these start-ups were led by industry outsiders, managers who lacked the required expertise and crucial relationships.

If the key proposition of the independent exchange was to create better prices through more competition, it didn't succeed. Many companies simply didn't want to trade with unknown partners. This should not be surprising, as most B2B transactions do not involve commodities. For that reason, most companies prefer to buy directly from a few prequalified suppliers, using long-term contracts to source products on favorable terms. A marketplace with lots of suppliers and buyers simply isn't the value proposition they seek. These companies may want price and product competition from time to time, but on those occasions a better option might be a reverse auction or the use of spot markets to generate information as a basis for negotiating new prices.

Another challenge faced by many independent exchanges was the low barrier to entry. In the chemical industry, for example, there were at least thirty electronic market start-ups, companies with names like ChemCross and ChemRound. Extreme competition among these new, independent exchanges killed margins, and ultimately led to the demise of many of them. Exchanges like Eumedix, Chemdex, and PaperX all failed to develop enough volume and liquidity in their markets to prosper.

To achieve long-term success, independent exchanges needed to deliver hard-to-replicate services for well-defined vertical or horizontal niches. The Pan European Fish Auctions, for instance, resolved major market inefficiencies. BuildNet, a construction exchange, likewise provided solutions for industry-specific problems such as job-lot scheduling and materials planning. PartMiner concentrated on hard-to-find components. CheMatch, meanwhile, is trying to differentiate itself by evolving markets to trade risk.

Some independent trading exchanges have found niches in relatively low-risk trading activities, such as bulk commodities and indirect materials. Others have partnered with major industry-sponsored consortia markets to bring focused capabilities to a particular industry. For example, the ingredient marketplaces Novopoint and Foodtrader.com provide specialized products and services to Transora, the marketplace sponsored by the packaged food and beverage industry.

As independent exchanges adjust to the changing competitive landscape, some are adding new capabilities, such as supply chain coordination, integration, and sourcing services. ChemConnect, for example, augmented its exchange through its purchase of Envera, which in turn improved the functioning of the chemicals supply chain by providing order tracking and monitoring as well as new capabilities for coordinating logistics, payments, and settlements. Similarly, SciQuest's expanded offerings to chemical companies now include software to manage chemical reagent assets throughout their life cycle. VerticalNet, meanwhile, provides software and services to connect suppliers to electronic markets more easily.

Strategically positioned independent exchanges will continue to play an important role in industry supply chains, but they will be limited to specific niches and will not be the dominant model for B2B electronic commerce.

Finally, it is important to note that one of the main strengths of independent exchanges is their potential neutrality. As shown in chapters 3 and 4, the value of markets can be unbalanced among sellers and buyers. A market might even be designed to favor one or the other. But independent markets can be designed in a more balanced way to provide value for both sellers and buyers.

## Consortia Exchanges

Soon after the emergence of independent trade exchanges, traditional industry players responded with their own electronic markets. In the U.S., more than sixty consortia-led electronic markets were created in the latter half of 2000, with equity investments averaging $8.5 million per consortium member.[3]

These consortia offered major industry players the opportunity to keep the benefits of online trading to themselves, rather than give them up to independent exchanges. Founders of these marketplaces typically represented a substantial portion of the industry's trading volume, thus marginalizing competitors. For example, the twenty-one founding members of Quadrem, the electronic marketplace for mining, minerals, and metals companies, represent two-thirds of the industry's total market capitalization and more than 25 percent of its buying power.

Consortia exchanges are generally buyer-driven. They create a common platform for buyers to work with multiple suppliers. In addition to simple search, matching, and ordering capabilities, consortia exchanges can provide substantially higher levels of benefits, including supply chain planning, collaboration, and order and logistics tracking. They also try to be the one-stop-shopping source for their industry, offering basic maintenance, repair, and operations products procurement, direct materials procurement and exchange services, price-comparison product catalogs, industry news, expert forums, and standards-establishing authorities. Some consortia are even setting up secure sites on which multiple companies can collaborate on engineering projects.

Although consortia markets are supported with adequate capital and guaranteed volumes from consortium partners and have been able to start up quickly, they have faced challenges. Covisint, the consortium exchange in the automobile industry, illustrates this.

Founded by such leading automotive companies as DaimlerChrysler, Ford, General Motors, Nissan, and Renault in cooperation with Oracle and Commerce One, Covisint is building a global electronic marketplace to link automotive companies with their suppliers. Prior to Covisint, Ford and General Motors were pursuing rival initiatives with competing vendors. Ford was building Auto-Xchange with Oracle as a strategic partner, and General Motors was building Trade-Xchange with Commerce One. This unusual consortium in an industry with intense rivalry among competitors and their software vendors occurred because the automotive suppliers protested the requirement to interconnect to multiple systems if they wanted to supply multiple automakers. To make matters worse for suppliers, DaimlerChrysler was setting up a third exchange in cooperation with SAP, the German-based enterprise resource planning (ERP) software provider.

By combining these initiatives into one major exchange, the automotive companies could reduce redundancy and provide suppliers with a more consistent standard for trading with different buyers. The large automotive companies could also leverage their purchasing power to save on key materials from their suppliers. With each of the three majors purchasing between $70 billion and $90 billion in goods and services annually, a small fraction of the purchases would generate billions in transactions through the exchange—thus creating huge savings for the car companies.

Despite its potential to revolutionize automotive supply chains, however, Covisint has grown slowly. It took over a year to find a CEO, for one thing. For another, both Volkswagen and BMW, the two major European buyers, have been reluctant to join the exchange due to confidentiality concerns. The need to satisfy rival consortium members also has slowed decisions, and the need to accommodate different members has added to development costs.

Despite the challenges, consortia will play a key role in industry supply chains for several reasons. For one, they effectively cut independent third parties or upstart dot-coms out of the game, leaving the consortia members with all the advantages. For another, the consortia are places where members can learn from one another, with minimal risk. Finally, from within the consortia, they are able to influence the adoption of XML and other critical trading standards.

## Private Exchanges

Private exchanges will have sophisticated electronic market capabilities, providing for deeper supply chain collaboration, more exchange of proprietary data, and fuller integration of a firm's business processes with those of its trading partners.

Seller-based private exchanges enable a company to provide added value to key customers. For example, Cisco's private exchange (the Cisco Connection Online) allows its customers to configure, place, and check the status of orders. This secure exchange enables buyers to customize the routers and other products they've purchased at minimal cost. For Taiwan Semiconductor Manufacturing Company, the private exchange allows geographically dispersed engineers to collaborate on chip-design projects, enabling more rapid changes to designs and reducing times to market.

Buyer-based private exchanges, on the other hand, try to make supply chain management more efficient and effective. At a basic level, they provide online ordering, product and shipment tracking, invoicing, and other basic functions. More sophisticated exchanges promote deeper collaboration, with capabilities for forecasting, supply planning, product design, exception management, and other functions. Wal-Mart, for example, provides its suppliers with access to two years of customer transaction data through its private exchange. The suppliers analyze this data to make recommendations for in-store product assortments, improved market segmentation, and inventory management strategies.

Cisco integrates both its buy- and sell-side exchanges. Its system allows critical order information to flow directly to key suppliers assembling Cisco products. This enables the suppliers to better forecast inventory and schedule operations. Cisco's exchange has enabled it to lower material costs by more than $170 million and reduce labor costs by $108 million.[4] The company was also able to cut inventory in half and double inventory turns. Cisco's private supplier exchange also allows the company to collaborate with suppliers in product design and even eliminate steps in new prototype and product development, thus reducing the time to market.

Companies with a dominant industry position or leading supply chain management capabilities sometimes build their own private exchanges. For example, Wal-Mart has already leveraged its buying power in this way. The benefits Wal-Mart can receive by using its own private electronic market are likely to outweigh benefits from an industry consortium. Its dominant market position ensures all key suppliers will participate in its private exchange, and Wal-Mart guarantees its supply chain advantages are not disclosed or dissipated on a shared-service platform such as a consortium exchange. In contrast to industry exchanges, private exchanges can be adapted quickly to the needs of specific trading partners without having to go through a cumbersome decision-making process. Private exchanges also enable companies to establish very secure connections to partners.

While we expect private exchanges to dominate B2B electronic commerce, they will not be relevant to all companies. Where supply chains are simple and already efficient, a private exchange may not offer enough new advantages. Alternatively, many small firms may not be able to afford private exchanges. In the latter case, a consortium approach may be more suitable. Even large companies with complex supply chains will have to carefully consider private exchange investments. Lower-cost alternatives could deliver equivalent results when the product life cycle is long, the number of customers and suppliers is small, and the requirements for engineering and coordination are simple.

Each of the three types of exchanges thus offers different types of value. Table 5-1 lists the key business functions electronic markets must develop to support supply chain activities.[5] We expect these capabilities to be distributed unevenly across exchange types.

## Plugging into B2B Electronic Markets

Plugging into B2B electronic markets is not easy. There is rarely a "one size fits all" market to meet a company's varied needs. Thus companies need to connect to a portfolio of electronic markets. In addition, they need to carefully manage the integration of electronic markets with their existing processes and systems. This often requires a dedicated organization.

TABLE 5 - 1

## The Electronic Market Portfolio

| Capability | Independent Exchanges | Consortia Exchanges | Private Exchanges |
|---|---|---|---|
| Community content | • | ••• | • |
| Procurement (indirect materials) | ••• | ••• | • |
| Procurement (direct materials) | •• | •• | ••• |
| Settlement and payment | ••• | •• | • |
| Fulfillment and logistics | •• | •• | ••• |
| Product development | • | • | ••• |
| Supply chain planning and collaboration | • | •• | ••• |
| Customer service and support | •• | •• | ••• |

- • Minimum capability
- •• Moderate capability
- ••• Strong capability

## The Portfolio Imperative

Given that different electronic markets have different strengths and capabilities, many large firms are taking a portfolio approach to fill their needs. The Dow Chemical Company, for instance, which makes more than 3,500 chemical, plastic, and agricultural products and services 170 countries, buys and sells through a portfolio of several B2B electronic markets. Some streamline internal purchasing. Others address external supply chain processes, interacting seamlessly with customers regardless of how they wish to do business with Dow.

Figure 5-2 illustrates the company's electronic market portfolio strategy, which is divided into six parts. The right side is the sell side of Dow; the left side is the buy side. The upper part of the figure shows the products related to Dow's

FIGURE 5-2

## Dow Chemical's Portfolio of Electronic Markets

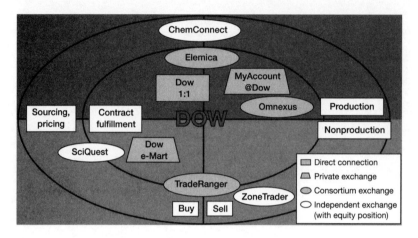

Source: The Dow Chemical Company. Used with permission.

production (primary processes). The lower part relates to nonproduction or secondary processes. The inner circle relates to critical products often sourced or sold via contract fulfillment.[6] The outer circle relates to products purchased via competitive sourcing and pricing.

Dow's buy-side electronic market participation and related initiatives include:

- **Dow 1:1**—A set of direct connections with select suppliers for the coordination and direct contractual fulfillment of strategic materials.

- **Dow e-Mart**—An internal buying tool with a multivendor catalog of nonproduction goods and services offered by prequalified suppliers.

- **Elemica**—Consortium electronic market for coordinating the purchase and contractual fulfillment of key production materials.

- **TradeRanger**—Electronic market for sourcing, pricing, and contractual fulfillment of nonproduction goods (pipes, valves, tanks, etc.). This exchange is primarily targeted to serving petrochemical companies.

- **ChemConnect**—Independent electronic market through which Dow sources and negotiates prices of raw materials when warranted. Using ChemConnect, Dow is able to make spot purchases of commodities and get greater visibility into industry supply and demand for commodity chemicals.

- **SciQuest**—An independent electronic market through which Dow acquires critical laboratory supplies.

Dow's sell-side electronic markets and electronic channel initiatives include the following:

- **MyAccount@Dow**—A customizable private exchange through which Dow's customers can order products and obtain account-related services.

- **ChemConnect**—Independent electronic market through which Dow auctions chemical products when warranted.

- **ZoneTrader**—Independent electronic market that allows Dow to clear excess information technology equipment.

- **Omnexus**—Consortium electronic market for plastics products and services that provides an additional channel for Dow's products.

- **Elemica**—Consortium electronic market for contractual fulfillment of chemical products and services used on both the buy and sell sides.

- **TradeRanger**—Consortium electronic market used for the disposition of excess nonproduction equipment and spare parts in the petrochemical industry.

Through these varied electronic markets, Dow is not only able to reach and serve customers better, but also to realize new efficiencies in procurement and supply chain planning and coordination.

## Managing the Integration Points

Implementing a portfolio of B2B electronic market connections is not easy. To realize the true value of electronic market initiatives, companies need to efficiently interconnect their legacy systems and business processes to the electronic markets and their other participants. As illustrated in figure 5-3, companies must manage a number of different integration points with different electronic marketplaces and other systems.

For example, on the buy side, the desktop procurement and enterprise systems of the buying organization need to interconnect to marketplace systems. Similarly, on the sell side, the supplier order management system, enterprise systems, and collaborative planning and forecasting tools may need to be connected to the marketplace. In addition, the marketplace must link to related financial service providers and with the legacy electronic data interchange systems of related buyers and suppliers. The number of actual integration points and the complexity of the integration challenge increase as new markets emerge and technologies change. As sourcing software and dynamic pricing tools become more common, these will also need to be integrated with the firm's B2B market initiatives.

Companies can integrate their business processes and legacy systems with those of an electronic marketplace in three different ways.

1. **Ad hoc interconnection**—Here, companies build specialized applications, connecting between a

FIGURE 5-3

**Alternate Integration Strategies**

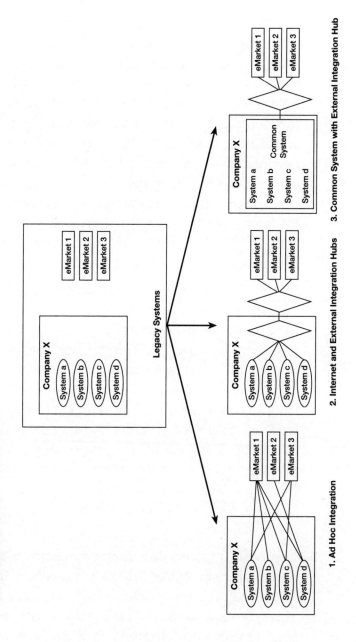

specific internal system and an external electronic market application as needed. But large companies often have many different ERP implementations that need to interconnect with each other and with multiple markets. Custom software that integrates across these different systems is both expensive to create and difficult to maintain. In the short run, the ad hoc interconnection strategy allows companies to integrate a specific legacy system and a specific electronic market quickly through a custom application. For large firms, however, the strategy does not scale efficiently, and it positions the firm poorly to connect to multiple electronic markets.

2. **Integration hub**—This strategy employs a dedicated system between the internal system of a firm and the external electronic markets. The integration hub connects to key points in the firm through custom interfaces, while linking to external electronic markets through the reuse of connectors. By centralizing all connections to a hub, companies can reduce redundant connections, boosting their ability to participate in multiple electronic market systems. By having an integration hub, companies minimize the changes required to their internal systems, thus reducing management and maintenance costs.

3. **Common systems**—This strategy attempts to reduce the number of required integration points by implementing a common system within the organization. This is typically done with well-defined interfaces that connect to the electronic markets. However, upgrading to common ERP systems is both expensive and time-consuming, and generally not suitable for large firms invested in legacy systems.

Given a choice between the three paths just outlined, we believe integration hubs will be the dominant integration strategy of firms that have substantial investments in legacy systems. Integration software platforms (such as webMethods) help companies implement integration hubs.

When W. W. Grainger, a leading provider of maintenance, repair, and operating supplies and business services, established two electronic markets (Grainger.com and OrderZone.com), it confronted a number of integration challenges. OrderZone.com provides a one-stop, online B2B procurement service where customers can purchase products from a number of suppliers with a single order and receive a single invoice. In order to meet its B2B integration goals, Grainger needed to find a way to connect Grainger.com and OrderZone.com to Grainger's existing SAP enterprise resource planning application. By using integration software like webMethods, the new marketplaces could provide customers with real-time information on pricing and availability of products directly from Grainger's internal system.

Furthermore, customer orders are automatically injected into Grainger's applications, eliminating the time and labor involved in rekeying data. In addition, webMethods B2B connects Grainger.com and OrderZone.com to other B2B marketplaces, enabling Grainger to be a featured supplier on those exchanges.

## Organizing to Realize Value

Seizing the value of electronic markets is not just a technical challenge. It's an organizational challenge as well, for several reasons.

For one, electronic markets disrupt the tacit and explicit relations between workers in the firm, their relationships with others, and the skills and processes required of them to work effectively. The new markets transform individual job roles and often require retraining or reassigning existing staff. As electronic procurement expands, for example, procurement managers and their staff will have to learn new skills—how to respond to dynamic pricing, how to hedge risks through futures, and how to manage purchases through multiple channels, among many others.

For sellers, electronic auctions may challenge long-standing personal relationships and traditional ways of working with buyers. Some people will be willing to be retrained. Others will resist or be unable to adjust to the new roles and forms of business relationships.

Electronic markets will also drive the need for new job roles, skills, and processes in the organization. Firms using sell-side electronic markets, for instance, will have to learn how to update their catalogs and other materials with the latest offers, prices, and information—all tailored to key customers. This will require new skills in catalog and content management software and even new security to protect proprietary information. Marketing, IT, and other parts of the organization will also have to make changes, ultimately finding effective working relationships between the sales, manufacturing, and information technology sides of the organization. Without the commitment of budget, staff, and executive attention to the above types of organizational and process transformation, companies are unlikely to realize the full value of electronic markets.

Given the novelty of electronic markets and the need for specialized skills, some companies are setting up dedicated organizations to manage their initiatives. When Dow Chemical recognized that electronic commerce would reshape their industry, they formed a corporate-level Electronic Business and Commerce Team to develop the company's strategic vision and drive implementation throughout the widely dispersed organization.

The team continues to collaborate with Dow's independent global businesses, balancing the benefits of a unified strategy and single infrastructure against the demands of each business's specific markets. This arrangement allows a certain amount of controlled experimentation through which Dow can learn by doing and establish tested capabilities. The company can then leverage these capabilities across the organization (where appropriate) to maximize the benefits achieved.

In addition to working within the current organization, the team creates and manages a portfolio of new dot-com business opportunities that provides Dow with external options that complement its internal initiatives. Dow's Electronic Business and Commerce Team was divided into several subteams to support increased focus and effective implementation of the key elements of the company's electronic commerce strategy:

- **Electronic Channel Team**—Collaborates with Dow businesses to evaluate electronic channel strategies.

- **Customer Interface Team**—Identifies customer needs and implements processes, technology, and organizational changes to deliver them.

- **Supplier Interface Team**—Identifies and implements strategies, processes, and technology that support interaction with suppliers.

- **Electronic Business Services Team**—Identifies and implements internal shared services.

- **e-Communications Team**—Provides integrated electronic communications capabilities to internal clients and to partners.

- **e-Business Development Team**—Creates and manages a portfolio of dot-com business opportunities.

These teams allowed Dow to assemble and deploy the specialized expertise required to effectively implement electronic market initiatives across their different business units.

In addition to specialized organizations that support expansion into electronic markets, executive champions are another key success factor. At General Electric, ex-chairman and CEO Jack Welch's personal support for the use of reverse auctions sent a message to the entire firm about his commitment to using this new tool. By giving credence and support to a good idea, Welch motivated its widespread adoption in the firm. In two years General Electric went from saving less than $10 million in auctions to saving more than $400 million.

Although many electronic exchanges have foundered, others are proving themselves capable of increasing the efficiency of multiple supply chain activities. But in chapter 6, we will see that exchanges can do much more than buy, sell, or trade new products. There are big markets to be tapped in resale products, refurbished goods, and even such intangibles as risk and knowledge.

# 6

## Using Markets Creatively

FOR YEARS, British Petroleum (BP) has been a leader not only in oil production, but also in oil trading. In 1998, Sir John Browne, the chairman and CEO of BP, took the idea of trading a step farther. Acknowledging that environmental issues were a pressing concern (and would constrain industry performance in the years ahead), Sir John pledged a 10 percent decline in the company's greenhouse gas emissions by the year 2010 from its 1990 levels. He also outlined an extraordinary means of accomplishing this goal efficiently: The company would use a flexible, Internet-based mechanism that would allow BP's diverse business units to trade emission rights and discover the cheapest ways to reduce overall emissions.[1]

The system works as follows. First the company set a baseline for emission rights (how much a unit could produce) at the 1998 level for each of its 150 business units. Next the company set a target goal for reducing carbon dioxide emissions in proportion to the baselines. Each business unit was then free to invest in emissions reduction directly or, alternatively, to purchase reductions in emissions from other business units that were able to reduce their volume of emissions or exceed their target emissions more cheaply. For example, if a unit with expanding production had an increased need for emission rights, it could use the electronic market to purchase rights from a unit that was reducing production or could cut emissions more cheaply.

Employing this system, BP traded reductions in 2.7 million tons of emissions in 2000 and has been recognized as the leader in greenhouse gas emissions trading. For BP, setting up an internal electronic market for emissions was not only a creative coup, but also superb business strategy. Sir John led the company efficiently to its emissions goal using the "invisible hand of markets."

British Petroleum's internal electronic market is only one strategic application of markets. Markets can also be used to:

- Improve returns from product resale
- Better manage business risks
- Generate predictions
- Acquire expertise efficiently
- Improve resource allocation and decision making within the firm

Markets have often been used in the past to trade tangible goods externally. However, as the British Petroleum and other examples in this chapter illustrate, in the future markets will increasingly be used to trade intangible goods as well as to improve internal processes, such as decision making and resource allocation. In the following sections we examine how companies can utilize markets strategically and realize value from these markets.

## Markets for Leveraging Resale Products

The proliferation of resale markets in the U.S. and elsewhere is nothing short of a cultural phenomenon.[2] Millions of people have emptied their garages and closets and dumped their secondhand wares onto numerous increasingly popular

Internet auction sites, eBay being the most prominent. Now secondhand shoppers can buy anything on the Web, from used Braun Aeromaster brewers and Beanie Babies to CAT scanners, restaurant equipment, and even robots. Market makers have proliferated as well, with names ranging from GolfClubTrader.com and MyNextBoat.com to TireDex.com.

The resale market is a boon for consumers, but for manufacturers it is proving to be a double-edged sword. On one hand, manufacturers can use resale markets to accelerate new product adoptions and trade-ups. But on the other hand, the resale markets cut into new product purchases. How will Braun, for instance, continue to sell new coffee brewers for $70 when used machines pop up on the Internet for less than $20? That's a tough question, and one that smart companies are trying to answer.

## Accelerating Markets

One answer may be that companies should simply encourage consumers to sell older products on the Web, take the proceeds, and use them to buy the latest products at the store— that is, accelerate product turnover. This strategy works, but its success depends largely on which of two curves a company's products are built—a long technology diffusion curve or a short one.

Widely used in marketing, technology diffusion models (see figure 6-1) describe the pattern by which innovative new products are adopted by consumers. One company might aim for the innovator segment with state-of-the-art products, while another might court the larger pool of adopters with lower-cost copycat products.

Products with a long curve are the best for resale. The reason is that the product will stay current for a longer time. The new Volkswagen Bug is a good example. The early adopters recognized that the resale market would be

FIGURE 6-1

**Standard Technology Diffusion Curve**

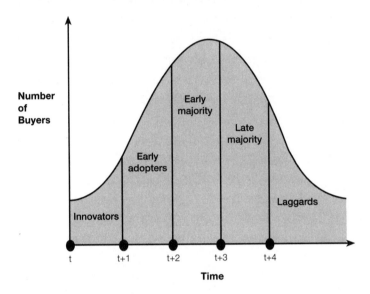

extremely good (probably from the initial rave reviews). They knew they might pay a high price (way over sticker price) to grab one, but the resale potential lowered their risk.

The story is different, however, in companies that create products with a high rate of obsolescence (see figure 6-2). Particularly in industries where product life cycles are measured in months rather than in years, the curve shift means that early followers will have to be very fast indeed to avoid obsolescence. Innovation will be rewarded more, and more often, as buyers find it increasingly easy and cost-effective to upgrade. For companies in industries with longer product life cycles (such as the makers of airframes and white goods like appliances), the opportunities may be even greater. Not only will online resale markets accelerate the demand for new goods, they will also offer ways to make new profits off the goods previously sold.

FIGURE 6-2

**Accelerated Technology Diffusion Curve**

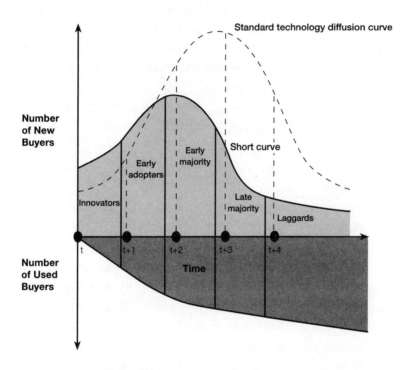

## Reselling the Goods

For some companies, then, it makes sense to create their own resale market to accelerate user adoption of new products. These sellers recognize that although a new sale occurs once, continuous product resale (with a commission) is the next best thing to an annuity. The automotive industry, for one, realized this a long time ago.

The used-car market is one of those resale markets that didn't need the World Wide Web: It is easy to gather enough buyers and sellers on a local basis, thus making the secondary market work smoothly. In fact, today the used-car market dwarfs the new-vehicle market in annual sales volume and beats its profit margins as well. How have the automakers capitalized on this situation? First, by taking trade-ins—but more profitably, by pushing leasing, an alternative made possible by resale markets. Car makers are also able to expand their customer base through this strategy. Those who buy factory-refurbished Lexuses at a discount, for instance, are likely to be a very different customer segment than those who buy the new car.

Dell Computer has also ventured into resale territory with its DellAuctions, a used-computer auction site. The obvious goal has been to get buyers into the new PC market much faster than before. Unfortunately for Dell, the site has stiff competition from eBay, Yahoo!, and Amazon, which have a far greater pool of used computers for sale. Because of this competition, Dell recently closed its United Kingdom site, although the U.S. site remains active.[3] Because computers have become such a commodity, with limited brand preference, it seems that Dell would do better to work with the markets with the greatest liquidity, rather than go it alone. Automobiles, on the other hand, are more brand-specific in the minds of consumers. Here it makes sense for manufacturers of specific brands to establish their own resale markets.

## Refurbishing Goods

If selling used goods makes sense, selling "refurbished" goods is a new move that may prove even smarter. It's being tried by a number of companies. Dell, for instance, has added an online refurbished-products outlet to their Web site, where returned and slightly used products are reconditioned and sold at a discount. Compaq, Hewlett-Packard, and IBM also sell refurbished goods.

The refurbishing strategy has a number of factors in its favor. One is that refurbishing is environmentally friendly, a fact lost neither on Dell nor on its many "green" customers (who cringe at the thought of thousands of PCs piling up in landfills). Although only 17 percent of the durable goods sold in the United States are recycled, we see several reasons for that number to increase. For one, sales of refurbished products can often earn higher margins than sales of new ones. Particularly for companies that already provide post-sale support and maintenance, the new liquidity offered by online resale markets makes getting into the refurbishing business a clear moneymaker.

Xerox is another visionary when it comes to refurbishing. By taking charge of its own secondary market, Xerox has done at least two smart things: captured the value of those recycled goods sales and protected its reputation by ensuring that the products being sold are in good working order. One lesson all companies that both create and refurbish products learn fast is the value of redesigning for longevity. This isn't simply a quality and durability issue; it involves anticipating how upgrades might be easily incorporated in a reworked unit. Xerox, for instance, found that a simple change in the design of its cartridge assemblies—changing some screws to snaps and putting reusable parts in more accessible places— would yield substantial savings on refurbishing costs. Another strategy is to design products in such a way that re-usable parts are specific modules in the design.

One major concern for any seller looking to organize a re-sale market is that consumers demand some measure of quality control. Dell has addressed this by extending its used-PC warranties to three years—the same coverage as its new products. The more a product changes hands, the more critical quality authentication becomes. Just as the tamper-proof odometer greatly improved the credibility of the used-car trade, similar safeguards will add to the resale value of other products.

## Retaining Value

Finally, sellers can embrace resale markets by targeting the opportunities that arise from extending the use of the product. For instance, increased involvement in the total life of a product means more frequent customer interaction and a stronger basis for ongoing relationship sales. Who is better positioned than a company that buys used goods to know when a customer is ready to buy a new item? Investing more heavily in branding is another strategy for retaining value in a world full of resale markets. The premium on branded merchandise, and the difficulty of selling unbranded goods—has always been great. But in online resale markets, where options are plentiful and future product performance uncertain, the preference for branded goods is amplified.

Every seller in today's economy should carefully examine these three opportunity areas (reselling, refurbishing, and retaining value) and learn how they can boost revenues and enhance profitability. Two capabilities are important to design with care: quality control and reverse logistics.

## Quality Control and Reverse Logistics

To benefit from the advantages of resale markets, companies don't have to jump into the business with both feet. An easier way is to offer buyers a trade-in option and then simply move the used equipment upstream using third-party services.

If a company creates "reverse logistics" capabilities, it can process the trade-ins that limp back two years after the sale just as easily as it processes the merchandise returned after two weeks (because of buyer's remorse or dissatisfaction). Of course, employing reverse logistics often requires the design and management of a new physical logistics network (including facility locations and inventory control).[4] Furthermore, the interaction between the forward and reverse flows of goods makes reverse logistics challenging to implement. One option is to outsource these activities to specialists, companies like Ingram-Micro Logistics and Genco, which focus on the return, recycling, and value salvaging of high-tech products.

Third parties can also refurbish many products as well as undertake quality assurance and product testing. In fact, customers don't even need to know that a third-party specialist is servicing and handling product returns.

## Beat Them at Their Own Game

Electronic resale markets create new managerial imperatives for controlling the value of goods and assets. But should you join them or try to beat them? Beating a resale market for your product doesn't mean stamping it out. In fact, forget that thought. This consumer-friendly genie isn't going back in the bottle. Rather, use competing resale markets strategically to:

- Accelerate markets and earn returns from products twice
- Enhance brand value
- Improve product designs
- Drive supply decisions
- Engage new customers

We have already seen how automakers like Lexus refurbish products, accelerate markets, and reach new customers who can't afford a new product. Now, consider the strategy put to work by Royal Doulton. As a producer of, among other things, limited-edition ceramic figurines, it's in the business of creating "collectibles" for which there will clearly be a secondary market. But does a company like this worry about those markets and their potential to divert new-product buyers to used goods? Not in the slightest. The company depends on these markets because they demonstrate the brand's ability to retain or appreciate in value—which justifies the company's premium price at original sale. Where would luxury-auto makers like Mercedes-Benz and BMW be without the resale markets to demonstrate their cars' worth? For various branded and luxury goods, resale markets bolster their prices, rather than diminish them. Thus, resale markets can be vital to making a brand.

Resale offers another possibility for manufacturers. By studying resale markets like eBay, smart manufacturers can learn how best to create new products that sell. Although electronic resale markets are new, companies have relied on prior designs to boost profits. Part of the brilliance in producing such "classic" products as Harley-Davidson motorcycles, Fender guitars, the new VW Bug, the Plymouth Prowler, Fossil wristwatches, and other trendy products is a recognition that people sometimes value the older, recycled models more than the new, "improved" ones. That's the whole story behind the relaunch of the Volkswagen "Bus," which has been designed to follow the lines of the famous VW vans of the 1960s.

VW is not alone. The Parker Pen Company, for instance, noted the passion with which collectors swapped their classic fountain pens from the 1920s and 1930s. Taking the cue, Parker (and Mont Blanc and several other makers) have come out with new lines of pens that look just like the originals—and operate even better. The surprising news is that Parker now commands a higher price for its new "classic" pens than the real, genuine 1920s issue. Similarly, smart managers will look to resale markets to inform the designs of the future.

Resale markets are also good barometers of market activity. For instance, the accumulation of inventory in the resale markets may signal a slowdown in new product demand. This was certainly the case when the Internet bubble burst and the nearly new equipment of the dot-coms poured into the resale markets at close to twenty cents on the dollar. That huge supply of used inventory was a harbinger of bad times for such new-equipment makers as Cisco and Nortel, which had to write off billions of dollars in unsold inventory. Despite the short-term pain, the existence of a thriving resale market is actually a good thing: In the case of the dot-com crash, for instance, the excess inventory might have taken longer to reallocate in the economy without the resale markets, creating a more sustained economic slowdown.

Resale markets are also good for building relationships with new customers. Cisco, for instance, recognized that when its equipment was sold used, the company tended to lose contact with the new owner. To correct this, Cisco started a program to encourage its used-equipment buyers to register their products, get software upgrades, and buy maintenance services. It was a move that brought Cisco into contact with a new pool of customers.

Resale markets will increasingly motivate buyers to manage the value of an asset over the asset's lifetime. As a result, companies will also invest in tools to help buyers take advantage of the greater salvage value for used products. Peregrine Systems software, which helps manage the value of products over a lifetime, and Peregrine's ZoneTrader, a major industrial resale market that maximizes the salvage value of used equipment, are two examples. Using these tools, companies will increase the utilization and productivity of technology and other assets.

## Markets for Trading Risks

*Could sw Dev risks be traded?*

As electronic markets proliferate, companies will increasingly seek to use markets to trade risks. In fact, electronic markets and the ease of trading may in themselves lead to higher price volatility, necessitating the need for risk management through futures and derivatives markets. The best competitors will strategically use emerging electronic markets to hedge key risks and realize superior value for themselves and their shareholders.

Among the airlines, for example, the top performers in the third quarter of 2000 were those that had best protected themselves against soaring energy prices.[5] According to earnings reports, fuel costs rose 64 percent at America West and 75 percent at US Airways. However, at Delta Air Lines fuel costs rose just 45 percent. The airline uses about 3 billion gallons of fuel a year, but by hedging, or finding ways to guarantee some of its fuel costs, the company saved $160 million during the third quarter—substantially more than any other airline.

How did Delta save more than its peers in the entire quarter? By hedging and trading the risk of price increases through the purchase of call options on heating oil (a product whose prices closely track those of airline fuel). The call options provided Delta with the option, but not the obligation, to buy heating oil at set prices. When jet fuel and heating oil prices rose precipitously in 2000, Delta was able to purchase heating oil at a fixed price and sell it for a profit to offset the increases in jet fuel costs. Thus the airline protected itself from unpredictable rises in fuel prices.[6]

## Trading Risk Is Not New

Trading risk is not new. In the twelfth century, sellers at medieval trade fairs signed contracts, called *lettres de faire*, promising future delivery of their wares at a fixed price. In the 1600s, Japanese feudal lords sold their rice for future delivery in a market called *cho-ai-mai* under contracts that protected them from bad weather or warfare. Futures contracts for commodities have been sold on the Chicago Board of Trade since 1865.[7]

Today, electronic markets expand the opportunities for those trading options, forwards, and futures to transfer risk from risk holders to risk takers (see "Options, Forwards, and Futures"). This transfer of risk between buyers and sellers reduces the overall risk in the economy, allowing the volatility of prices confronted by any one party to be diminished. Many manufacturers trade these instruments to manage input price variability for metals and other commodities. Others trade these instruments to manage volatility and risk in foreign exchange rates, interest rates, output prices (such as a farmer selling a contract for his future crop at a fixed price), or input risks (such as Delta's hedging to control fuel costs).

As electronic markets proliferate, better price histories will be generated to understand the volatility of prices. Data from multiple trades will create sequences of prices for the commodity or asset being traded, and these can be correlated to prices of a basket of stocks of related commodity products (or to the price of a related asset that is traded in futures or options markets). If there is a strong and consistent correlation between the asset whose price risk you wish to trade, and a commodity or stock that is widely traded, it becomes feasible to hedge your risk using the derivatives on the basket of stocks or futures and options on the commodity. This was Delta's strategy for trading jet fuel price risks, and we expect more firms to adopt similar strategies.

In Delta's case, fuel is the second largest expense after salaries. Unhedged fuel is 16 percent of Delta's total operating costs. It is not only a large expense, it is also a very volatile one. Over 1999 and 2000, unhedged fuel fluctuated from 38 cents to $1.01. Jet fuel costs rose above $1 per gallon in October 2000.

To protect against price increases but still benefit from declines, all without paying huge amounts for this sort of insurance, Delta purchased call options on heating oil. This gave

## OPTIONS, FORWARDS, AND FUTURES

Options, futures, and forwards are called derivatives because they derive their value from the value of some other asset, which is precisely why they serve so well to hedge the risk of unexpected price fluctuations. Derivatives cannot reduce the risks that go with owning volatile assets, but they can determine who bears the risk from speculation and who avoids it. Options are contracts that give the buyer the right, but not the obligation, to purchase or sell something at a later date at a price agreed upon today. Forward contracts are agreements between the buyer and a seller to purchase and sell something at a later date at a price agreed upon today. In contrast to options, which need not be exercised, parties to a forward contract incur the obligation to ultimately buy and sell the good. Futures are contracts traded on a futures exchange to buy or sell something at a future date. Futures contracts evolved out of forward contracts and are like liquid forward contracts. Unlike forward contracts, futures are traded on organized exchanges called *futures markets* and are subject to a daily settlement procedure.

the airline the right, though not the obligation, to buy the heating oil at set prices on given dates. In purchasing these options and developing the hedge, Delta looks at, say, a ten-year period to find the average cost of the fuel and then tries to buy options that lock in the price within a narrow band of the average price. It's a perpetual program, and the company likes to cruise at 50 percent of purchases hedged. Hedging is not free, and any time Delta buys an option, the downside is the premium. However, in five quarters between 1999 and 2000, for $100 million in premium expenses, Delta has netted more than $600 million due to hedging. In part, Delta benefited from laying down a lot of hedges when prices were at an all-time low—especially in early 1999.

Thus, Delta uses hedging because the company thinks it's the right thing to do to manage a very volatile and large expense. As Delta CFO Michele Burns stated: "The watchwords in our program are risk management and simplicity. Delta has been very aggressive in this area; we try to stay very much ahead of the curve."[8]

## Making Markets for Trading Risk

Until October 2001, Enron seemed to illustrate the profitable leverage of risk management expertise.[9] Enron was formed by the merger of two natural gas pipelines in 1985. With initial revenues of $10 billion, the company grew to become a diversified global energy company with $40 billion in revenues by the year 2000. In the 1980s, Enron and its predecessors faced substantial margin pressure as the natural gas industry was deregulated, squeezing profits in the gas value chain. Deregulation also led to greater price volatility and a shift from purchasing through direct contracts to buying 75 percent of natural gas through spot markets.

In 1989, trying to satisfy the needs of a customer who wanted a fixed-price natural gas contract, the Enron negotiating team devised an innovative solution of a swap. Basically, the customer would pay Enron a fixed fee over a period of time. As market prices varied, Enron would then pay floating prices to natural gas providers and transporters. In this relationship, Enron would bear the risk if the floating prices rose above the fixed price. But Enron correctly guessed that prices would fall over time.

This innovation led to a broader strategy of building a gas bank in which pooling across many contracts would let Enron offer fixed-price contracts at minimal risk. These gas contracts could be treated as securities, that is, turned into financial instruments and traded like corporate bonds and mortgages. While natural gas contracts would cover less than 10 percent of all natural gas traded, they would account for about two-thirds of corporate bonds, mortgages, and gold contracts specified on a long-term fixed basis. In effect, securitization of these contracts created new financial instruments and a new high-growth, high-profit business for Enron.

Based on these successes, Enron brought its risk management and market making expertise to new areas. In 1999 it developed EnronOnline[10]—an Internet-based global transaction system. EnronOnline was an over-the-counter, principal-to-principal private exchange, rather than a public exchange subject to more stringent regulatory requirements. The system allowed buyers and sellers to view real-time prices from Enron's traders and transact instantly to purchase various commodities.

Enron acted as a principal on all transactions and generated credit risks and automatic limits for all parties participating in the system. By acting as a principal, Enron had primarily set up a private risk management solution for all participants rather than a market where all parties are free to trade with each other. Online trading in North American and Nordic electricity as well as in coal, pulp and paper, and plastics began in December 1999; online trading in gas and power in the rest of Europe and in most of Enron's other trading categories—weather products, crude oil and refined products, petrochemicals, and emissions rights—began in January 2000. More recently, Enron sought to make futures markets for computer memory chips.

By Enron's calculations, by summer 2001 it was by far the world's largest electronic business in terms of transaction values. Most of its profits came from its trading operations, and it was the world's premier market for trading electricity and natural gas contracts. But beginning in October 2001, Enron unraveled as a company, and it filed for Chapter 11 bankruptcy protection in December 2001. Enron's fall began with a restatement of its profits for prior years and a $1.2 billion reduction in shareholder equity due to questionable partnerships with the participation of a key company officer. These partnership structures allowed the company to transfer losses and debt off its balance sheet. Disclosure of these practices and the lack of transparency in Enron's accounting or its various trading positions led to a loss of confidence in the company's creditworthiness by investors, creditors, and companies it traded with. Its share price dropped precipitously, and the company ceased trading operations as it sought bankruptcy protection to reorganize.

As noted in chapter 2, the success of markets is predicated on trust and confidence. Enron's accounting practices and failure to properly disclose its earnings destroyed this trust and led to EnronOnline ceasing operations—as traders no longer trusted that Enron, as a counterparty to each trade, could meet its obligations. As the company reorganizes, it sold key EnronOnline operations to UBS Warburg, a bank with a high creditworthiness rating.

To date, other B2B online markets have provided only limited futures, options, and risk-trading capabilities. However, efforts are being made by B2B markets to expand into futures and risk trading and to create neutral marketplaces in contrast to Enron's private risk management model. CheMatch and the Chicago Mercantile Exchange (CME), for example, are collaborating to create a neutral, regulated futures market for basic petrochemicals such as benzene.[11]

Launched on October 19, 2001, this exchange works the same way as futures for agricultural commodities on the CME, such as beef and pork bellies. For example, each benzene contract represents 42,000 gallons of product, and prices are measured according to an index compiled by DeWitt & Co., a leading chemical industry consulting firm that tracks pricing, supply, demand, and other industry conditions. A buyer purchasing a future at 75 cents per gallon for November "maturation" can sell that future at any time before November. The contract is settled in cash according to the index price when it matures.

If the price is 80 cents per gallon at the time of maturation, the contract holder gains 5 cents per gallon. Alternatively, if the price at maturation is 70 cents, the holder pays a premium of 5 cents a gallon. These chemical futures are bought and sold on CheMatch's site as well as on CME's electronic trading system, Globex2. CheMatch and CME are in discussions with overseas exchanges to set up futures trading in Asia and Europe. Clearing is through CME's Clear21system.

In contrast to regulated futures, companies that provide private exchange systems, like Koch Industries and Shell Chemicals Risk Management (Scrim), provide a more complex range of financial derivatives. These include fixed-price contracts or financial "swaps" as well as price caps, floors, and "collars," which set both upper and lower price limits for petrochemical and plastic products. These risk management providers take a financial position on every transaction. In contrast, a separate buyer and seller are matched on each regulated futures deal at CheMatch.

The providers of both futures and risk management services say that futures are a way to protect against price cycles. In contrast to standard futures contracts, private risk management can be more costly. Some estimate that Enron's cost was as high as 2 to 3 cents per pound of material covered. On products such as polyethylene, selling for 35 cents per pound with a very small margin, that is a high price to pay. Futures markets and risk management offerings are still in their early stages. To succeed, they will have to create liquidity and bring major producers on board. This will be tricky, as some producers are concerned that petrochemicals could go the way of other commodities, where the price is influenced more by financial speculators than by the actual trades of the product. However, other producers say pressure for a predictable earnings flow will drive producers to use such instruments over the next five years. The emerging trading on CheMatch and private risk management systems suggests there is a bright future for trading futures and other similar instruments.

The securitization and trading of risk is appropriate not just for commodity products. One widely cited example is the issue of celebrity bonds—bonds that are backed by future royalties and receipt of a celebrity's work. In 1997, rock star David Bowie was a pioneer, selling $55 million in bonds backed by future royalties of his recordings. For Bowie, the deal enabled him to raise cash on terms more favorable than a bank loan, and without the downside risk of not being able to pay back the loan.

All the bonds were purchased by Prudential Securities and were rated triple A by Moody's Investors Service. Despite the possibility of creating such asset-backed securities to transfer risk on many comparable assets, few similar issues have followed. David Bowie was tailor-made for the deal—he owned the rights to every song in his catalog of some twenty-five albums—but that turns out to be rare in the music industry. Building a security on an artist's work that is distributed across multiple studios would be very challenging. Furthermore, banks are likely to profit more from providing loans to artists, secured by their royalty stream. The royalty streams and hence risks can then be pooled and converted into a security with less overall risk, one that the bank could sell for a better premium.

## Using Markets to Trade Risk Wisely

Costly mistakes from inappropriate hedging and speculation are well known. These include spectacular failures such as the Dutch tulip mania between 1630 and 1637, when futures markets encouraged speculation that drove tulip prices toward unsustainable prices in the thousands of guilders per bulb. More recently, in the 1990s, several major companies including Procter & Gamble, Gibson Greetings, and the German Metallgesellschaft AG made blunders in the use of derivatives. As Peter Bernstein recounts in his classic book on risk,[12] many of these firms sought to use derivatives to trade currency and interest rate risks. But their managers seemed to have forgotten the most basic rule in investment theory: You cannot expect to make large profits without taking the risk of large losses. For example, instead of hedging against interest rate risks the managers often sought to increase earnings by speculating on the direction of future interest rates. When interest rates went the wrong way the companies incurred major losses.

When and how should managers use markets to trade risks? All risks cannot be traded efficiently. Operating risks are often best mitigated through careful process design and monitoring. In contrast, markets are most appropriate for trading risks associated with the price of inputs and outputs. They are especially useful when:

- Input or output prices are highly volatile.

- Input components are highly specialized, there are few or no alternative suppliers to mitigate the risks, and the cost of delivery failure is high.

- Outputs are specialized to a customer.

Hedging is a bet that bad things will happen in the market. However, as at Delta, hedging is not free; managers must weigh the expected benefits of owning derivatives for hedging against the costs of creating and trading the derivatives. Hedging strategies are especially inappropriate when:

- Input and output prices are not very volatile.

- The commodity being hedged and the underlying asset contract are very different and not strongly correlated in price.

- There are quantity risks offset by natural hedges. For instance, a farmer does not know and cannot hedge the uncertainty of the size of his crop. Due to weather conditions, the crop size could be small when prices are high or large when prices are low. However, the weather creates its own natural hedge against quantity risk. All farmers in the area are likely to face the same conditions. When the farmer hedges, the price volatility no longer offsets the uncertainty of the crop size. Thus, hedging in this case can actually increase the overall risk.

- Investments are motivated by speculative profits or savings rather than professional risk management and risk reduction.

When contemplating trading risk, managers must address a number of challenges. First and foremost is the need to ensure enough liquidity in these markets. If regulated futures trading is to take off, settlement systems and adequate financing must be in place to provide traders with guarantees that obligations will be met. Markets for trading risk work only if the market for the underlying product is fairly liquid. Risk management strategies that assume *ex ante* the existence of liquid markets in which to hedge and remove risks lead to pressure on the underlying markets and reduce market liquidity precisely when it is most needed. Thus managers must carefully select the markets in which they participate and track the level of liquidity in the corresponding product market.

Both market makers in risk and market participants will require risk management systems. For example, Enron claimed it had extensive back-office systems and other policies to manage risks. Sophisticated risk management software was used to track its risk exposure across products and markets in real time. The company also maintained a staff of more than 100 people who constantly evaluated and managed risk by unit, geography, and projects. According to Jeff Skilling, a former CEO, these controls enabled Enron to always manage its exposure to risks (not making one-way speculative bets) "such that they are never out of balance more than plus or minus one percent." The company's select investments in various parts of the vertical value chains in natural gas and other industries in which it made markets also helped the company understand supply and demand forces at play as well as operational details to assess risk in key segments of a value chain. This provided information advantages to the firm.

In addition to risk management systems, firms trading risk must also consider the compensation policies for its traders. Many firms compensate their traders based on the percentage of profits they make. This potentially creates a huge agency risk where traders have every incentive to make very large bets on one side or another. If the bet goes their way, they get a huge bonus. If it goes against them, they leave and get a job somewhere else, maybe a raise as well. To reduce these risks, compensation policies should discourage very risky trading and bonuses should be based on the overall performance of the firm.

At present, most organizations do not have the capabilities required to effectively hedge various inputs and outputs.

Critical risk management systems and processes will have to be established within companies. Where hedging can substantially reduce critical financial and input risks, new organizational relationships will be required such as between procurement and CFO and treasury functions. Since this is likely to be costly, we initially expect specialized third parties to provide risk management services until companies develop the skills to participate in broader markets.

## Markets for Generating Predictions

Attendant to risk is uncertainty, or the absence of information about what will happen in the future. In addition to enabling the trading of risks, markets can be powerful information-processing mechanisms that aggregate the views of multiple market participants to generate a prediction of the future.

In many ways stock markets fulfill this role, where investors take all available public information, process it, and through their trades construct a price for the stock of a company. This price reflects the beliefs about the company's future earnings at any point in time. Market mechanisms can be utilized to aggregate information from multiple informants to generate predictions for future. Online virtual futures markets have been used to predict outcomes ranging from political elections to football games. Early experiments with virtual markets for prediction show promising results and can be used by companies to forecast sales and test the market potential of new products. We'll consider the following three examples:

- The Iowa Electronic Markets (IEM)

- Artificial markets for sales forecasts

- The Hollywood Stock Exchange

## The Iowa Electronic Markets

The Iowa Electronic Markets was one of the first Internet sites to attempt to generate predictions.[13] This market opened for trade in June 1988 and sold shares in the candidates for the U.S. presidential election—George Bush, Michael Dukakis, and Jesse Jackson. In this market the value of the share in a candidate after the election was defined as their share of the popular vote. At the beginning of trading, the participants would spend $1 to buy shares in all the candidates. Traders would then sell the shares of those they expected to lose and accumulate shares of those they expected to win at the prices they felt would be profitable. This market was remarkably accurate. On the eve of the 1988 election it forecast 53.2 percent for Bush and 45.2 percent for Dukakis, which was within a margin of error of less than 0.2 percent, compared with a margin of error of the final opinion polls of 2.7 percent.

Started as a teaching tool by the University of Iowa's Tippie College of Business, IEM has become a serious forecaster of U.S. and foreign elections. In 1992 it again correctly forecast the Clinton victory within two-tenths of a percentage point, far more accurately than opinion polls. Polls typically try to take the electorate's pulse by asking whom a participant would vote for if the elections were held that day. In contrast, the IEM provides participants with pecuniary incentives and opportunities for clear gain and loss based on their prediction. Thus each trader on IEM is betting on an election's outcome based on his or her specific knowledge.

The market aggregates this information to generate a price and a prediction. How does this work and why might it be more accurate than polling? Polls typically have poor predictive power because individual preferences for a candidate can bias the forecasts and overestimate the likely popular vote for the respondent's preferred candidate. But would these biases carry over to the electronic marketplace? An analysis by Forsythe et al. as described by Hal Varian suggests a reason why biases are less likely to influence outcomes.[14]

In this analysis, it is proposed that a few "marginal traders"—those who submit limit orders close to the market price—are most responsible for driving the market price. These traders typically have twice as much investment in the market, are more disciplined in trading, are willing to unload shares if the prices go too high, and make more frequent trades. An examination of the trading processes of marginal traders showed no evidence of judgment biases.

Although the IEM has had a good track record, it isn't always right. It failed to pick the winner in Mexico's recent presidential election. The exchange did poorly because only twelve people wagered, too few to create a viable market. Like the rest of the United States, it was also confounded by the year 2000 presidential election. On the day before the election, the futures for George Bush dramatically increased in price, suggesting a Bush victory and dominance of the popular vote.

Ultimately Bush did win, with a little help from the Supreme Court, but Al Gore won the popular vote. Why might the market have failed? Some researchers suggest the number of market participants was too small to accurately reflect the sentiments of voters in a close election. Alternatively, the participants in the markets may not have reflected the diversity of U.S. voters and may not have been adequately informed about the intent of different voter groups.

Today the Iowa Electronic Markets trade a number of futures. For a mere $5 sign-up fee, users can log on and open an account with a maximum deposit of $500.[15] The most popular markets are winner-take-all: Each share in a winning candidate pays $1, but losing shares are worthless. To get started, users first must buy all the candidates in a race for $1. Then they sell the candidates they expect to lose for whatever price they can get. The price—40 cents, say, for each $1 share—rises or falls depending on how other people are betting. This technique is used to process and estimate the most likely outcome of an election.

Artificial markets are also being used within corporations. An application at Hewlett-Packard illustrates their use in forecasting sales.

### Sales Forecasting at One High-Technology Company

Sales forecasting is a challenging problem in most organizations. Through their customer relationships, salespeople often have the best knowledge of the customers and their likely purchase patterns. However, there is typically an agency problem. As salespeople are often compensated on the basis of commissions and bonuses for exceeding a specific quota, some may choose to underestimate their likely sales to a company. This way they are likely to exceed their quotas and receive their bonuses. However, this underestimation can create problems with production.

Charles Plott, a leading experimental economist at the California Institute of Technology, and Kay-Yut Chen created an artificial market for forecasting sales. The system works as follows.[16] While any particular salesperson might have very little information, the collection of salespeople might have considerable knowledge. Critical knowledge for planning and operations is dispersed in the opinions, hunches, and beliefs of its sales force. Artificial markets were set up to collect and organize this knowledge. Ten markets were created and operated within the company. The markets were labeled SEP-LOW 000–1500, SEP-LOW 1501–1600, SEP-LOW 1601–1700, and so on.

If the upcoming September sales of the item were to fall in the interval 1501–1600, then the market with that label would pay $1 per share to the owner of the shares, while all the other markets would pay nothing, and so on. Each person who was allowed to participate was given an endowment of approximately 20 shares in each of the markets. The markets were open for several days, during which participants could buy and sell shares, thus reflecting their beliefs about the likely level of sales.

The question posed was whether the market prices would reflect the relative probabilities of the actual sales. Since the prices must range from 0 to 100, they can be interpreted as probabilities. Thus, the price of 9 in the market SEP-LOW 000–1500 can be interpreted as the "market belief" that the probability is 0.09 that the September sales will be in the range of 0–1500. The exercise was conducted sixteen times inside the company, and the mean state was never further from the actual sales than was the official prediction; it was significantly closer in all but one. "All indications are that this type of mechanism works in practice," concludes Charles Plott.

Prediction markets generate information and provide signals to resolve uncertainty about the future. Much like the stock market can be a leading indicator of the economy, artificial markets are emerging to help generate information for resource allocation decisions in different industries. Another example of such a market is the Hollywood Stock Exchange (HSX).

## The Hollywood Stock Exchange

This exchange, at http://www.hsx.com, started in 1996 as a gaming site that converted films, music, television, and celebrities into shares of virtual stock.[17] Instead of investing real money in company stocks, customers invest with free Hollywood dollars (H$) in movies, stars, and musical artists. But the goal of the customer is the same: buy low, sell high. The goal of the exchange was to attract millions of movie fans with the thrill of trading and leverage that interest into dollars—and eventually, into investments in film ventures. This business model, which relies on advertising and encourages players to view ads in exchange for Hollywood dollars, has not worked very well. But independent research has shown that the HSX forecasts of movie success, award winners, and the success of individual actors are highly accurate.[18] In February 2001, HSX created HSX Research to analyze and sell data from the exchange to buyers within the entertainment industry.

The exchange works as follows. Customers register for free and then get 2 million H$. They buy and sell shares. As more people buy shares, the value of a film property or celebrity increases. After four weeks in release, a movie's stock delists and cashes out: Shareholders receive H$1 per share for every $1 million that the movie has grossed in the U.S. Thus the stock price reflects the traders' prediction of performance: Traders buy shares they feel are undervalued and (short) sell those they feel are overvalued. Currently there are more than 400,000 registered users. Predicting Oscar winners is based on options: The winning option pays H$25, the others, zero. Closing option prices reflect the market's assessment of each actor's probability of winning.

In 1999, HSX players correctly picked Oscar winners in eight out of eight categories, and in 2000 each actor with the highest final price won the Oscar. In contrast, the *Wall Street Journal* polled actual Academy voters, but only got 7 out of 8 correct. The site also forecast the overwhelming success of the indie flick *The Blair Witch Project*. Recent research by David Pennock and his colleagues shows that prices of securities in Oscar, Emmy, and Grammy awards correlate well with actual award outcome frequencies, and prices of movie stocks accurately predict real box office results.[19]

## Implementing Prediction Markets

Although today prediction markets are in the early stages of development, they promise to be a very important technique for eliciting the beliefs of different experts or members of a firm about the future. Managers will have to identify the most critical application areas for these markets, such as sales forecasting, product design, evaluation of new technology developments, or some other category of information. They will then have to evaluate the likely benefits and relative accuracy of market-based strategies for aggregating information and beliefs to generate predictions in contrast to existing mechanisms.

Over time, managers will more often use these mechanisms to resolve key uncertainties and to generate predictions and new business information. In a world where knowledge is widely dispersed in the organization, markets will be an efficient way to reveal the true preferences and beliefs of individual traders and experts. Markets provide more incentives to traders to yield this information, and the price mechanism is an efficient way to collectively assign value to beliefs.

However, the information and signals generated by markets are not perfect; they only reflect the best social consensus of participants. Examples in practice and laboratory experiments indicate that markets can make mistakes. To improve the information generated, companies creating in-house online markets for prediction must ensure several factors: that there are enough traders in the market (critical mass); that those traders represent the peer group that is knowledgeable about the issues the market seeks to address; and that there are sufficient incentives to motivate participants to trade and generate useful information.

## Markets for Knowledge

Online knowledge markets are still a novelty, but we believe more knowledge markets will be established in the coming years. Why? Detailed, thorough knowledge will be scarce, and therefore there will be a market for it. New technologies enable us to buy and sell knowledge. It will not be easy, but it will happen.

This trend started with digital information exchanges like Knexa.com (short for the Knowledge Exchange Auction), where users may buy and sell their knowledge and experience. They focus on downloadable knowledge items such as research papers. On the public site, you may post a question, and a seller or expert may respond. A buyer may offer a bid (in cash), which the seller may choose to accept. The buyer may then download the information and is subsequently expected to provide feedback and a rating of the seller. Ratings are made public. Knexa gets 20 percent of any fee. This type of exchange has two limitations: The value of the information must be communicated to the potential user before purchase, without giving away the knowledge itself. Also, the knowledge must be downloadable.

Despite these restrictions, several knowledge exchanges are now mature marketplaces. Keen.com, for example, is a Web site and phone service that provides live advice on any number of topics. Common discussion areas include medical advice given by doctors, tax advice, and venture capital advice. Keen makes its money by scraping 30 percent off the total fee the phone counselors get for giving their advice.

The business model is simple. There are advice seekers and advice speakers. The seekers use either the phone or the Internet to find an advice speaker. All speakers are given a rating on a scale of 1 to 5, based on past performance. Once connected, the seller is charged a per-minute fee, which is then shared by the speaker and Keen. Further bolstering

Keen's position is its business-method patent, granted in April 2001, for a system connecting advice-seekers with self-proclaimed experts via the telephone.

Keen.com can be categorized as a generalized question-and-answer exchange. More specialized exchanges, such as Experts Exchange (www.experts-exchange.com), focus on specific topics, especially in IT. Points are used as a currency, but since they can only be exchanged for novelty items (such as t-shirts), their value is mainly in tracking, not in illustrating the true value of different types of knowledge. Whether sites of this general nature can generate enough revenue to keep going is uncertain.

Optimism seems to be greater for more focused exchanges—intellectual property exchanges such as Yet2.com and the Patent & License Exchange (www.pl-x.com). On the latter site, users can bid to purchase patents and licenses, thus uncovering the value of an intellectual property. Some of these exchanges have become part of a broader intellectual asset management service offered by consulting firms.

Intellectual capital exchanges like eLance.com also create markets for knowledge. eLance.com is a professional services marketplace for Web-based projects used by businesses worldwide. It works as follows. Someone posts a project—for example, a request for a market research report. Potential providers then bid to perform that project, listing their credentials and how much they would charge. The buyer chooses the winner (usually the lowest bidder). eLance takes 7 to 10 percent of the seller's fee as a service charge.

eLance's projects work best in fragmented markets for tasks that can be delivered via the Web, fax, or e-mail. Projects tend to fall in into one of three categories: technology, from programming to Web design; creative design, from logos to corporate brochures; and business services, from translations to data entry. In February 2001, eBay and eLance linked their Web sites. In March 2001 the handheld computer manufacturer Handspring launched an online marketplace through which its developers, partners, and service providers could do business. Software development is a pressing matter for makers of PDAs such as Handspring's Visor. The demand for such devices is strong, but application programmers for them are in short supply. eLance runs this site.

As with the exchanges described in chapter 5, knowledge exchanges are finding that in order to succeed, they must add services focused on corporate needs in, say, customer relationship management, as revenue from advertising is insufficient to support public exchanges. In addition to its public exchange, Exp.com now provides solutions enabling customers to get their questions answered in real time by the appropriate company sales or service people.

Knexa also has an intranet version of its product in which providers earn points when uploading content and can earn additional points if others in the firm use the information. The points can be converted to prizes, comp time, etc. These services diverge from a classic exchange or auction model, but they provide much-needed revenue for the service providers.

If we analyze knowledge exchanges in terms of the market processes, it is clear that in order to succeed, a knowledge exchange must provide the following components:

- **Routing (solving the search problem)**—An efficient way to bring seeker and provider together, as well as to determine if the information is already in the system.

- **Pricing (solving the valuation problem)**—A way to value knowledge quickly and accurately, in a way that both the knowledge provider and knowledge seeker can accept. For example, this could be an auction for questions and answers, in which higher offers for an answer would presumably lead to quicker and better responses.

- **Rating (authentication) of both the knowledge and the knowledge provider**—How well can the information and the provider be trusted to be correct *and* relevant? How do you compare different potential providers?

- **Payment and settlement**—If a knowledge exchange uses "funny money" for pricing, how does that convert into cash or other things of real value to the users and the market maker? How do you ensure that seekers pay and providers are rewarded? This is a big issue with the public knowledge exchanges such as Experts Exchange.

- **Representation, regulation, dispute resolution**—How can you represent the product without giving it away? How do you resolve regulatory issues around copyright and ownership? How do you resolve disputes when the asset has already been used?

- **Incentives to gain critical mass**—How can you get people to share their valuable knowledge and their time?

In short, opportunities for knowledge exchange and value creation from knowledge sharing are myriad; solutions, so far, are few.

## Markets for Decision Making and Efficient Allocation

In capitalist economies, financial markets have been used extensively to efficiently allocate capital to firms in the economy. Today the power of electronic markets can be used inside the firm for efficient resource allocation and decision making.

Think back to John Browne and British Petroleum. The challenge was to identify the best ways of achieving target emissions reductions in a large and decentralized company. Knowledge about the best ways to reduce emissions lies within the business units and not at a centralized location. The electronic trading system BP created in cooperation with the Environmental Defense Fund helped BP solve this problem efficiently.

The intranet-based trading allows different business units to both offer and purchase emission rights. The system allows those who want to purchase rights to enter a bid, and those who want to sell to put out an offer. Sales occur when bids and offers match. The system allows BP to collectively determine the price of abating emissions. For example, in March 2001, emission rights traded at close to $20 per metric ton.

To make this market, BP had to do a number of things well. First it had to estimate its prior and current emissions, and this information had to be verified. Next, divisions needed to have a clear and tangible financial penalty for not meeting their emissions targets, either by acquiring emission rights or through savings generated from investing in improved technologies and processes to reduce emissions. These savings also had to be monitored and verified to build trust in the market. Thus, while internal markets may allocate resources through the "invisible hand" and the collective decision process of the market, like all other markets, they require regulation and authentication processes for building trust.

The principles of markets can be applied to a number of different problems in a firm, from investments in R&D and innovations to venture opportunities. However, as with emissions rights, there must be authentication mechanisms that assure that the seller has valid rights to sell.

We stand at the brink of bringing electronic markets within the firm for better resource allocation and decision making. Not all companies will be able to do this, however.

Markets require managers to give up some of their authority to the "invisible hand" of many decision makers. Fortunately for BP, it has a leadership and culture that supported this initiative. Indeed, despite its overall size, BP is designed to have a "human scale." Each business unit has its own unique set of objectives and provides an environment that fosters personal loyalty, a sense of belonging, and a desire to truly make a difference. The emissions trading market was consistent with this decentralization.

As multinationals get even larger, leaders will confront the choice of how to manage diverse operations and yet achieve consistent corporatewide goals. Instead of imposing a one-size-fits-all solution, select electronic markets will support more decentralized and effective decision making. Indeed, their use may be critical to making these large firms nimble enough to compete with smaller upstarts. Ultimately the leadership choice for CEOs will be to decide when the tyranny and certainty of the "visible hand" is better than the freedom of choice and uncertain outcomes of the "invisible hand."

# 7

---

# Market Tactics

IN 1815, WHEN Napoleon Bonaparte built a new army and prepared to attack the British, the British financial markets were full of gloom. After nearly fifteen years of fighting Napoleon's armies, they knew the British government was nearly bankrupt. Furthermore, they doubted that Wellington, the British general, could win the coming battle. Reflecting these prospects, British government bonds were selling cheap.

But Nathan Rothschild, the great financier, wasn't about to be swayed by market speculation. Instead, he assembled a flock of carrier pigeons on the French side of the channel. As Wellington defeated Napoleon at the battle of Waterloo, Rothschild's pigeons raced to England with the news. Acting on that information, Rothschild bought British government bonds at rock-bottom prices—turning a tidy profit when the news finally reached London the following day.

Like Rothschild, today's successful arbitrageurs also recognize the critical importance of information. Just as a small object can leverage a larger one in nature, so can a small amount of critical information create significant advantages in the markets. It is these asymmetries of information, in fact, that often determine which players will win and which will lose.

## Information Leverage

Today's electronic markets create particularly good opportunities for information leverage. In a sales auction, for instance, a seller can analyze the behavior of bidders, turning that analysis into a demand curve that anticipates what consumers will pay for a particular product. Likewise, an electronic market may be set up to segment its buyers by personal and demographic data, thereby mining the market for important clues to personal and regional tastes. In these ways, Internet auctions are providing new means of leveraging information. But the sword cuts both ways: The new electronic markets are also more transparent than the traditional markets, which can undermine information leverage opportunities buyers and sellers have had in the past. In electronic markets, all of the parties can have similar information about pricing, demand, and other variables of the trade. Therefore, everyone must rethink the existing information leverage opportunities and create new ones.

Markets and auctions structure the exchange of information between buyers and sellers. The market rules for revealing buyer and seller preferences and needs, their willingness to pay, and offer prices can have a major impact on price outcomes, and therefore who leaves or takes the money on the table. In this chapter we will show you how to leverage market information—such as the price consumers will pay for a particular product—to your best advantage. We will describe the differences between naïve and rational bidding and explore what has been learned about the behavior of bidders. We will explain how collusion is used to illegally throw auctions. And we will describe the psychological traps that plague many bidders. Finally, we will discuss the three areas that market players must focus on to succeed: informed bidding, strategic bidding, and the ability to advantageously leverage information.

## Building and Leveraging Customer Information

Today's electronic markets, unlike traditional ones, have the ability to customize offers instantaneously and inexpensively. This can be used to push market prices to their upper limits. Egghead.com, for instance, used this to its advantage in selling scanners. On July 24, 2000, Egghead put fifteen Agfascan 1212u color scanners up for bid, with a starting bid of $9.[1] Thirteen bids came in, up to $45, with a median price of $27. The next day Egghead.com released a virtually identical model, the 1212p (with a parallel rather than a USB port). This time, the company limited the number of units to six, with a starting bid of $25. All six were purchased, significantly raising the average price per unit. The first auction showed Egghead.com what bidders seemed to be willing to pay, so it could raise the starting bid for the second auction. By limiting supply (six rather than fifteen), it successfully cut out some of the lower bids.

Four days later, Egghead.com released twenty-seven Agfascan scanners at the "Smart Deal" fixed price of $36.99 (no auction). Although this was $10 above the median price of the auction of a few days earlier, customers were willing to pay it, perhaps to bypass the auction process and its uncertainties altogether. In the following weeks, Egghead was able to get an even higher price by releasing for auction only one scanner, while increasing the suggested bid. The high bid was $54, twice the median price of units sold July 24. Once Egghead had figured out its customers' willingness to pay, it leveraged that knowledge to get the highest prices the market would accept. This type of information was also used in Egghead's direct marketing efforts: Those participating in the Egghead auctions without winning were e-mailed an offer for a similar product—with a price close to their bid. This strategy was superb: Rather than the 2 percent conversion rate of most direct-mail pitches, Egghead's was a hefty 30 percent.[2]

Several other companies are beginning to use auctions to strategically plot the potential customers' willingness to pay. Ahold, a global food retailer and food service operator, for example, has been able to glean information about suppliers from its reverse auctions via the World Wide Retail Exchange platform, in which they receive reliable information about the potential suppliers' willingness to sell at a particular price.

## Bidding Strategies

Bidding processes in the English auction and other traditional auctions are set by well-established rules specifying the number of bids a bidder may enter, the sequence of the bids, and the order of allocating auctioned lots to buyers. As procedural rules and auction types vary widely, there are a number of strategies for bidding effectively in auctions. But electronic exchanges have increased the number of available bidders and bid takers that can participate, which, in turn, has changed the game considerably.

For one thing, the Internet and increased competition among bidders in emerging exchanges can be expected to eliminate much of the margins above the private value (see "Private Value, Common Value, and Surplus"). Thus in sealed-bid auctions, as the number of bidders increases, the optimal bid strategy is to reveal your true value immediately. So it is key to have a clear and accurate private value for the desired item, whether it is a good, service, or contract.

In reality, bidding in auctions is not that simple. A number of factors can complicate the pricing and bid-revelation process, from psychological pitfalls to strategic behaviors. Furthermore, bidders are rarely entirely rational, and actual bidding strategies run the whole gamut, from naïve to solidly rational.

### The "Naïve" Strategy

In consumer auctions we often observe what we call the "naïve" bidding strategy, where a bidder, desperate to win, bids up an item's price beyond its true value. In a study of early airline ticket auctions we found that the winners often could have paid less if they had gone to a consolidator. Naïve bidders often act as if they do not have a clear idea of the market value of the goods. Instead, they bid to win.

A more rational bidder would gather information and prices on comparable products, use this information to estimate a private value, and bid in a way that does not exceed the bidder's private value or the common value for the good. However, in many cases it may be very difficult to estimate a reasonable private value—especially for one-of-a-kind goods, or when the price cannot be determined due to lack of critical information.

### The "Mimicking" Strategy

The bidder may adopt the riskier strategy of mimicking a "reputable" bidder. In this strategy, one carefully selects a bidder with a reputation as an unusually savvy estimator and simply mimics his bidding behavior. Just before an auction ends, the "mimicker" outbids his mentor—and wins. Of course, this strategy is possible only when the identities of the bidders are known. Although this is not often the case, sometimes the seller will reveal the identities of the buyers to bring the competition to a boil.

### Multiproduct Strategies

When multiple products are sold through auctions, bidding often becomes even more complicated. When buyers have presold some of their products to wholesalers, for example, they must either meet the "book" or potentially lose face with their clients. In order to fill a book, bidders may have to exceed their private valuations on some products, subsidizing those losses with earnings on other items.

In those cases, what determines the bidding level is not the private valuation of a single item at one moment, but the surplus across multiple goods over the lifetime of the relationship. Industrial buyers may also complicate such bidding strategies by having confidential information about the private valuations of the nonparticipants. Instead of relying on their own private valuations, then, they will bid the private valuations of those to whom they can subsequently resell the goods, minus a profit for themselves. By reselling the goods, they move to a common-value situation (see "Private Value, Common Value, and Surplus").

### English Auction Strategies

The English auction is a sequential, ascending auction where each successive bid is higher than the prior bid. The winner is the person who offers the last bid, and therefore the highest price. As the English auction allows bidders to reveal their preferences sequentially, the effective bidding strategy for the winner is to add a small increment to prior bids until there are no more competing bids. In this case the surplus to the winner is the difference between their private value for the item auctioned and the price of the winning bid. In some circumstances, it may be beneficial in an English auction to use a "jump bidding" strategy to signal commitment. Instead of adding a small increment to a prior bid, one adds a large increment. The intent is to scare away potential other bidders. This phenomenon is seen in takeover battles.[3]

### Sealed-Bid Auction Strategies

Sealed-bid first-price (or second-price) auctions, on the other hand, are not sequential. In these cases, because so little in-

---

**PRIVATE VALUE, COMMON VALUE, AND SURPLUS**

*Private value* refers to a bidder's personal valuation of the object being auctioned—that is, how much the buyer is willing to pay for the object, or the minimum price at which the seller is willing to part with the object. *Common value,* on the other hand, refers to the value at which the good is commonly sold. In the case of mineral rights from a tract of land, the expected value of minerals that can be extracted from the land should be "common" to all bidders. A distinction that is sometimes made between private- and common-value auctions is whether the item is being purchased for personal use (private value) or resale (common value).

A bidder's *surplus* is the difference between the price paid and the bidder's private or common value for the item. It can be positive or negative, depending on how well he bids.

---

formation is revealed in the auction prices, economists have shown that the best strategy for every bidder is to bid close to their private value.[4] This is especially true as the number of bidders increases.[5]

In a second-price or Vickrey auction, the winning bidder is the one who bids the highest price, but the winning price is that offered by the second-highest bidder (second-price). Thus the highest bidder pays the second-highest bid. As with first-price auctions, the optimal strategy for bidders in this auction is to reveal their true private value.

### Lurking in the Wings: A Successful Bidding Strategy

Although bidding has many theorists, all with their favorite strategies, sometimes the most pragmatic is the most successful. Hal Varian, dean of the School of Information Management and Systems at the University of California, Berkeley, and one of the world's most influential theorists on the network economy, explains how this was true in one particular auction—the Santa Fe Double Auction.[6]

The auction was created in 1989 by three academics and was based on rules used by the Chicago Board of Trade. They decided to invite rival researchers to contribute software that would compete against others' programs in this digital auction house. IBM agreed to sponsor a $10,000 prize for the designer of the most successful software agent.

Thirty programs were entered: fifteen from economists, nine from computer scientists, three from mathematicians, and one each from an investment broker, a team of cognitive scientists, and a marketing professor. The virtual gavel for this auction tournament dropped in March 1990. Who won? Scott Kaplan, a clever graduate student in economics. "When I asked why he thought his program did so well," says Varian, "he responded that all the other contestants wanted to show their theory was correct. As a poor graduate student, he really wanted to win the $10,000!"

The prize-winning auction agent was, Varian says, "simple, nonadaptive, nonpredictive, nonstochastic and nonoptimizing." This is surprising, because one would expect that the winning strategy could adapt to uncertain conditions, predict the winning value, factor in the probability of certain bidding outcomes, or provide the optimal bid given certain market rules. But that was not the case. The winning strategy was to lurk patiently in the background while others did the negotiating. Then when the "bid" and "ask" prices got close, the program jumped in to steal the deal. It achieved this through a formula that waited until rival bids and asks came within 10 percent of each other, and then sneaked in a bid slightly greater than the previous ask.

After 28,000 plays, the graduate student's software strategy achieved almost total domination of the auction market. But the victorious strategy had an unfortunate downside. Before long, the market crashed. "The reason," Varian says, "is that a 'wait-in-the background' strategy only works if there are many other active traders. When the student's strategy took over the entire market, it could no longer get a free ride on price discovery by other bidders." Was the experimental auction software a model of ingenious simplicity, or a dark vision of the future of the Internet economy? On such questions hang the prosperity of little dot-coms and industry Goliaths alike.

## Bidding in Practice

As electronic auctions proliferate, more is being learned about bidders. Accenture's experience in running reverse procurement auctions shows that bidders quickly learn to assess their private values and bid accordingly in the compressed time frame of an auction. They also learn to recognize that they must have a clear idea of supply and fulfillment costs prior to bidding.

How do bidders typically bid in reverse procurement auctions? Initially, those new to an auction market bid tentatively near the start price (usually set at about 10 percent above the average prior procurement cost). Then bidders typically break through the initial price range to a new level and continue until the lowest offer is found and no lower prices are bid (figure 7-1). As bidders learn from prior auctions, they approach the expected close price more quickly so as not to waste time discovering the final price range (figure 7-2).

## Bidding Agents

As online auctions proliferate, several online tools are evolving to support the bidding process. Some of these add convenience to the bidding process, while others provide insight and decision support for the setting of private and common values. For example, Liquidation.com provides three auction tools: Buyer Alerts, Power Search, and Proxy Bidding.

Buyer Alerts allow the bidder to track and return to open

FIGURE 7-1

## Bidding over Time: The First Wholesale Frozen Vegetable Auction

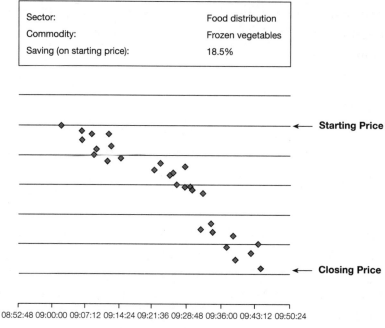

| Sector: | Food distribution |
| --- | --- |
| Commodity: | Frozen vegetables |
| Saving (on starting price): | 18.5% |

auctions that are of interest to the bidder. It is an intelligent monitoring and "single-click" bidding tool. Bidding on multiple items is efficient and timely, because Buyer Alerts send bidders information tailored to their interests, and bidders can increase their bids with a single click. Power Search is designed to help locate rare or hard-to-find items, goods that become available again after a shortage, or items that one had bid on in the past but lost. Proxy Bidding is a tool that automatically monitors an auction and will bid for the bidder during the auction. The bidder specifies the maximum bid, which is kept confidential. The bidding tool enters the lowest possible winning bid. If another buyer bids,

FIGURE 7-2

## Bidding over Time: A Later Auction Finds the Closing Price Range More Quickly

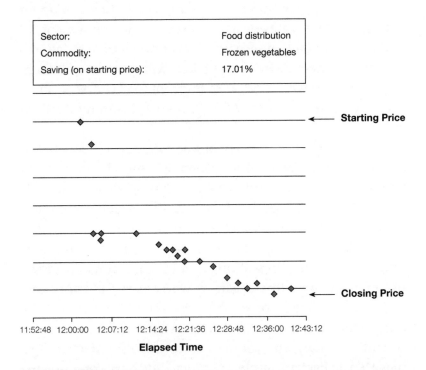

| Sector: | Food distribution |
| Commodity: | Frozen vegetables |
| Saving (on starting price): | 17.01% |

←—— Starting Price

←—— Closing Price

11:52:48  12:00:00  12:07:12  12:14:24  12:21:36  12:28:48  12:36:00  12:43:12

**Elapsed Time**

the bidding tool will automatically raise the bid until the tool user is winning again or until the maximum bid is reached.

While Buyer Alerts and Power Search are dedicated solely to Liquidation.com auctions, other search agents help bidders find items sold across a range of auctions. We expect other tools to be developed that will help buyers and sellers set their price ranges and better estimate their private values and costs.

## Psychological Traps and Strategic Misbehaviors

Even the best bidders can fall prey to a number of psychological traps. These include the winner's and loser's curse, anchoring and adjustment, and collusion risks.

## The Winner's and Loser's Curse

The winner's curse often arises in common-value auctions. In such auctions, a common value is ascribed to the item up for bid. Oil-drilling leases or wireless spectrum auctions, for instance, should have approximately the same value for all bidders. But in these cases, some bidders will overpay, quite simply, in order to win.[7] A good example of the "winner's curse" occurred in the August 2000 German telecommunications auctions.

In this case, Germany held auctions to license wireless spectrum rights for its third-generation mobile phones system—a system that would provide high-bandwidth Internet connections. The auction raised $46 billion from six consortia, with Deutsche Telekom the primary winner. Shortly after the auction, however, a key member pulled out of the winning consortium, complaining that the price it had paid was too high. As investors began to worry that the companies had paid too much for the licenses, the share prices of the other winners began to fall. Such was the winner's curse.

Unfortunately, the winner's curse can also affect companies that expect to receive products and services from the bidder. This has been the case in recent information technology contracts, where the winning bidder has won with a low bid that has not realistically estimated the costs of fulfilling the contract. When this happens, the bidder is forced to reduce the levels of service in order to retain their margins. Thus, the "curse" falls on both the successful bidder and the clients.[8] The winner's curse, however, can sometimes be a rational strategy, one that gets the company's foot inside the door, so that they can renegotiate once they get better information. This strategy is called "low-balling."

The loser's curse, on the other hand, occurs when a bidder regularly bids below what an optimal strategy would recommend—and thus regularly loses.[9] This might be due to risk aversion or some other conservative tendency; regardless, the bidder still bids less than he could afford—and less than his private value. In this case, the bidder doesn't win, but could have won with a more aggressive strategy.

Bidders can limit such losses if they come into the bidding with a good estimate of the private value of the item and a clear assessment of the costs of the purchase. Where accurate initial estimates are not available, as in the case of IT outsourcing contracts, bidders need to mark up a project twice—once to correct for cost underestimation on the projects they win, and a second time to include a profit margin.

In a similar fashion, bidders who want to avoid the loser's curse should build an accurate account of their costs. Once that is in hand, they will be able to bid more aggressively. Accurate information is the key in both cases; the more information the bidder has about his own preferences and cost structures (and the preferences and cost structures of the other bidders), the lower the risk of either overpaying or missing out on the deal.

## Anchoring and Adjustment

Sellers often set a trap, called anchoring and adjustment, that boosts the prices buyers are willing to pay. Consider a typical restaurant wine list. By having a number of expensive wines on the list, the restaurateur makes the medium-priced wines look like a good value. In essence, he's anchoring and adjusting the price the diner is willing to pay for a bottle of mediocre wine.[10]

Professors Joe Nunes of the University of Southern California and Peter Boatwright of Carnegie-Mellon University found a similar effect in automobile auctions. They analyzed the sales records of 1,477 antique cars at an auction. While the cars normally sold at a price close to blue book value, Nunes and Boatwright found that when the first of two cars sold at 100 to 200 percent higher than its blue book value, the subsequent car sold for an average 39 percent more than its blue book value. In other words, the greater the margin over blue book value on the first car, the greater the price differential one could expect for the second car.

This element of human nature, explain Nunes and Boatwright,[11] can help sellers in many ways. Retailers who position "impulse buy" goods at the cash registers, for instance, may want to add expensive items to the mix, making buyers feel more comfortable choosing the moderately priced products.

## The Problem of Collusion

Collusion is another potential problem in auctions and markets. As electronic markets proliferate, more price information becomes public. This information makes it easier for buyers or sellers to set similar prices. Collusion occurs in many different ways. For example, on some eBay auctions, two bidders illegally team up, one entering a low bid, and the other a very high bid (that no one can top). Later, the high bidder withdraws his bid and the sale automatically goes to his low-bidding collaborator. Called *shilling,* this ploy is also used by sellers, who use shills to enter fake bids, thus driving up the price.

Collusion undermines the participants' trust in the market. To prevent shilling, auctioneers develop and use monitoring systems to detect unusual patterns of bidding. In procurement auctions, auctioneers can also diminish collusion by carefully controlling the participants in the auction—as well as the information revealed to the participants. A good tactic, for instance, is to vary the prequalified group of bidders and hide their identities from other bidders. This encourages competition among the sellers and diminishes the possibility of collusion. Only the buyer need know the identity of all bidders.

## Three Steps into the Future

In the ongoing shift from place to space, we believe that most firms will soon be suppliers to or buyers of services from an electronic market. Some will even become market makers. In order to participate in these new markets, companies must focus on three key skills.

### *Master the Information Leverage Opportunities*

We believe that smart firms will increasingly use auctions for information leverage. They will use auctions to assess the customer's interest in certain products and their willingness to pay for them. They will also use auctions to gauge the price sensitivity of different customer segments. In dealing with consumers, information leverage will give businesses a greater edge than ever before. On the other hand, in business-to-business auctions, buyers also will be increasingly savvy about prices. However, sellers can analyze the buyer's willingness to pay for their goods. To be competitive, therefore, both sellers and buyers have to master information leverage opportunities.

### *Become an Informed Bidder*

As auctions drive markets to greater efficiency, bidders must learn to accurately estimate the private and the common value of the products they want to buy. Just as automobile blue book prices guide buyers to a common value for cars, so companies that sell in procurement auctions could adopt activity-based costing systems and invest in real-time cost information. This will help companies determine the true cost of servicing customers, and thus the lowest reasonable price they should charge.

Gathering cost information is not free. Companies will have to make new trade-offs between the value of gathering information about costs and customer value against the risks and potential losses from inefficient bidding. However, investments in gathering accurate cost and price information to determine private and common values can also help companies and bidders avoid the winner's and loser's curses.

For instance, if an auto parts company feels it must bid low to maintain a relationship with a carmaker, it must carefully evaluate the value of that relationship and decide whether bidding low continues to make financial sense. It might be better, for instance, to drop the relationship rather than continue to lose money by underbidding.

### Learn to Be a Strategic Bidder

You don't need a Ph.D. in game theory to maximize value in simple auctions. The key is to determine a private value prior to the bidding—and then don't bid beyond that price. As the number of bidders increases, the surplus any bidder takes away from an auction will diminish. Thus, for many procurement auctions, we expect that the competitors should bid close to their private value to increase their likelihood of winning. As bidders learn to bid more expertly in procurement auctions, we expect they will reach the equilibrium price more quickly. We also expect that several new software tools will become available to support the bidding.

As markets proliferate, they will demand new skills from managers and market participants. Some, like financier Nathan Rothschild, will master the art of taking advantage of information. Those who don't will lose. In the next chapter we will examine how to seize the value of markets in a dynamic and competitive electronic environment.

# 8

---

# Dynamic Market Strategies

MARKETS ARE RARELY STATIC. The Internet and improvements in the information technologies that motivated the transition from place to space continue to foster changes in electronic market processes, structures, organization, and governance. As technology improves and value decreases for relatively simple functions such as market access, search, and trade-matching services, both market makers and participants will have to thoughtfully navigate technological and competitive changes to the market space. How should market makers compete, and who should own markets in different stages of a market's life cycle? In this final chapter we outline the dynamics of the different types of markets as well as strategies to navigate changes profitably.

## Value Migration and Market Maker Strategies

When new markets are first introduced, the market maker's primary challenge is to get the new market to critical mass— a sufficient number of buyers, sellers, or both to create ongoing trading among participants. But the challenges do not stop there. The next goals are to grow and sustain the market, staying ahead of new entrants who may use even newer technologies to provide market services more cheaply or to create more value for customers. Technology relentlessly

179

improves, and the threat of newcomers to the market forces existing market makers to constantly review and renew their strategies and their offers to customers. Even established markets must pursue some crucial strategies to survive, grow, and sustain value. These include market differentiation, creating market networks, mergers and acquisitions, and leveraging market competencies.

## Market Differentiation

Electronic markets can renew their value proposition to buyers and sellers in numerous ways. Consider early B2B electronic markets. Many independent electronic markets were created with the simple proposition of expanding access to buyers and sellers and finding better prices through more competition. Likewise, consortia exchanges thought they could do much the same for key industry players and avoid handing over the returns of market making to a third party. Alas, given the low costs of market entry, this was not the winning value proposition they had hoped for. In order to survive, both the independent and consortia exchanges realized they had to deliver more than mere search and valuation activities. They had to provide collaborative forecasting, planning and coordination of production, and product inventory and delivery. To survive, many market makers— SciQuest, VerticalNet, and CheMatch among them—subsequently transformed their offerings to differentiate themselves from competitors. SciQuest added software to manage chemical reagent assets throughout the life cycle of use; VerticalNet became a provider of software to help suppliers connect to electronic markets more easily; CheMatch created futures markets in commodity chemicals.

As technology improves, the easy stuff becomes commonplace, and value migrates to other sources, such as solving the harder problems in trading. Many of the B2B electronic markets discussed throughout this book show that basic search and valuation for simple or well-defined products do not usually give market makers a sustainable advantage. In the process model we specified in chapter 2, increased competition and improvements in technology drive the value of markets toward more complex activities such as logistics, payment and settlement, and risk management. In rare cases, such as PartMiner and Bandwidth.com, search remains difficult for complex or hard-to-find products. PartMiner exploits this problem by building markets for hard-to-find electronics components. These types of independent markets are specialized, and thus serve a niche.

Another strategy for value creation and differentiation is to expand or transform the services and transaction mechanisms provided to buyers and sellers. Increasingly, markets are shifting from monolithic trading mechanisms to all-in-one markets that offer "one-stop shopping" for different trading mechanisms to suit the varied needs of customers. When eBay acquired Half.com and introduced the "Buy Right Now" feature, it increased the purchase options available. These new features allowed buyers to forgo the opportunity cost of participating in auctions. Today, 11 percent of the company's revenues come from these new mechanisms for serving customers.

Similarly, ChemConnect and numerous other exchanges provide multiple transaction mechanisms, and both the Dutch flower auctions and various stock exchanges are introducing new ways of meeting the special requirements of buyers and sellers who transact large blocks of inventory. The Dutch flower markets have introduced a brokerage service to match buyers who want to purchase flowers in volume from specific growers. HarborsidePlus is trying to create value by introducing a new mechanism for anonymous trading of large blocks of stocks, thus catering to the special needs of mutual funds and large firms. The New York Stock Exchange is also trying to introduce new methods that would allow mutual funds and other large entities to trade directly and rebalance their portfolio positions without adversely affecting the market price through their trades.

Electronic markets will increasingly give customers what they want, how they want it, and generally, when they want it. All-in-one markets will provide buyers and sellers with multiple ways of trading. This "frictionless" switching among trading methods will create new value. All-in-one markets recognize that preferences for trading methods may vary at different times for different customers. By offering a variety of transaction methods, we expect all-in-one markets to give customers fewer reasons to leave, thus raising both revenues and customer loyalty (see "All-in-One Markets—The Early Evidence").

Market makers who offer multiple transaction models on the same electronic market platform recognize that customers have different volume, risk, and effort preferences when trading. Some customers are risk-takers who will expend considerable effort to find a good price in an auction. Others are not willing to waste their time, preferring instead to buy directly from the electronic catalog for a fixed price. Customers' preferences may also vary over time.

For example, I may pay a full fare for air travel as a reimbursable business expense, but use Priceline's name-your-price for an optional weekend trip to another city. For that reason, airlines like American and Lufthansa offer a variety of different fares and transaction mechanisms to benefit maximally from the variety of customer preferences. Meeting a wide range of needs is not easy. To maintain consumer trust, all-in-one market strategies must be implemented with care so as to not confuse the customer with too many choices and too wide a spread of prices. All-in-one markets will work to the extent that they can create a sufficient amount of trading activity across all the mechanisms offered. But to be successful, they must also create new value and convenience for customers.

---

### ALL-IN-ONE MARKETS—THE EARLY EVIDENCE

Companies already recognize the value of offering customers multiple ways to buy and sell. A 1999 Accenture Institute for Strategic Change survey of more than 300 major Web sites identified a number of different mechanisms for customer interaction, as shown in table 8-1. On average these sites offered two different ways for consumers to purchase goods and services. As illustrated by the chart in figure 8-1, more than 66 percent of companies had more than one mechanism. In addition, the static catalog was the most popular transaction mechanism, constituting 28 percent of all mechanisms. Auctions comprised about 16 percent of all mechanisms.

In short, the survey shows that companies recognize that giving customers choices for conducting transactions is increasingly critical to winning and keeping them.

All-in-one markets are implemented in two ways: either internally, by incorporating multiple trading methods within the organization's market, or by creating seamless connections to external marketplaces that provide alternative trading methods. Business portals and electronic procurement software (such as Ariba) exemplify the latter by giving different vendors of the same product or service a common interface for multiple transaction methods.[1]

---

To be competitive, market markers must master strategies other than differentiation.

## Partnering and Alliances

As we saw in chapter 3, two of the key factors for success in markets are critical mass and liquidity. As a market expands with the entry of new buyers and sellers, positive externalities benefit each individual participant as well as the market. In rare cases, underlying technologies or services cannot

**TABLE 8 - 1**

## Types of Transaction Mechanisms Used by 320 Commerce Sites

| Mechanism | Definition |
| --- | --- |
| Static call | Online catalog |
| Dynamic call | Online catalog with continuous price/attribute update |
| Product tailored | Offerings tailored to meet individual customer specifications |
| Price tailored | Prices change based on purchase history/loyalty |
| Reverse | Buyer posts desired price for seller acceptance |
| Spot | Buyer and seller bids clear instantly |
| Negotiation | Technology-supported negotiation |
| Seller auction | Buyers' bids determine final price of seller's offerings |
| Buyer auction | Buyers request price quotes from multiple sellers |
| Barter | Buyer and seller exchange goods |
| Continuous replenishment | Ongoing fulfillment agreement under special terms |
| Bundled | Seller combines multiple products into a pre-packaged offering |
| Bulletin board/clearance | Offerings limited by availability of product or discount |
| Partnership | Integration of seller processes with those of buyer |
| Referral | Link to nonowned mechanism/commercial Web site |

scale and may even degrade with additional participants, or increased competition diminishes margins. But generally, expanding the user base is critical to sustaining value to all the other participants. One strategy for doing this is to form partnerships and alliances.

In many B2B electronic markets, for instance, competitors are increasingly sharing trading platforms and establishing new ones to enable competitors to coordinate their end-to-end supply chains. Transora, the industry-sponsored food and packaged goods exchange, for example, was originally formed by a group of companies that would normally com-

FIGURE 8-1

**Frequency of Each Transaction Mechanism as a Percentage of Total**

*There is no dominant approach to exchange across industries. The most frequently used mechanism by far, the catalog, made up only 28 percent of all mechanisms observed.*

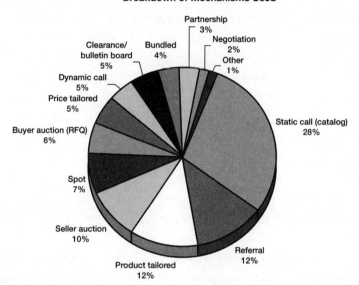

**Breakdown of Mechanisms Used**

Partnership 3%
Negotiation 2%
Clearance/bulletin board 5%
Bundled 4%
Other 1%
Dynamic call 5%
Price tailored 5%
Static call (catalog) 28%
Buyer auction (RFQ) 6%
Spot 7%
Seller auction 10%
Referral 12%
Product tailored 12%

pete in purchasing and other supply chain processes. These companies included Unilever, Earthgrains, Coca-Cola, and Procter & Gamble. But in forming Transora, they collaborated in catalog purchasing, bidding and price quotes, online sourcing for raw materials, packaging supplies, and other critical goods and services. In the future, the exchange plans to add other supply chain processes, such as collaborative planning and demand management, flow management, order fulfillment, customer service, new product commercialization, and relationship management.

Transora has established alliances with two other exchanges—Novopoint.com and Foodtrader.com—to expand its offerings. Novopoint is a neutral B2B transaction and information hub for buyers and sellers of food and beverage ingredients. Foodtrader.com is a global procurement marketplace for the food and agricultural industries. This alliance expands the access of Transora members to even more critical supplies. At an operational level, these alliances enable more seamless transactions for Transora members across multiple markets, as well as the formation of joint standards. In addition, Transora has formed alliances with the GlobalNetXchange. The latter is a consortium of leading food and packaged goods retailers, including Carrefour, Kroger, Coles Myer, and Sears. Again, this alliance connects key exchanges, linking both buyer groups and suppliers across the value chain.

For Transora, the alliances effectively move it toward a megahub—a central marketplace providing interconnections to other markets that link to competitors, buyers, suppliers, and companies that provide complementary goods (see figure 8-2).

Cooperative alliances within and across industry marketplaces allow many electronic markets to deliver the requisite variety of services and achieve a sufficient scale to compete effectively. Alliances among dominant cross-industry incumbents serve to expand their user base and diminish the threat of competitive entry.

## Mergers and Acquisitions

Mergers and acquisitions are another way of expanding the user base and responding to technological change. Market making is expensive, with high fixed costs for the purchase and implementation of complex software, the acquisition of customers, and the attainment of critical mass. And although variable costs continue to drop, the economics of the market still encourage mergers to share the fixed costs among a

**FIGURE 8-2**

**Transora's Evolution to a Megahub**

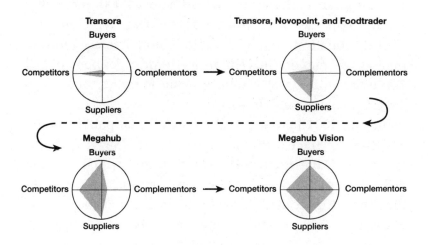

larger user base. Mergers also allow market makers to realize economies of scale and better serve customers by giving them access to a wider range of products and trading opportunities, regardless of their location.

Consider Electronic Communication Networks (ECNs), such as Island and Archipelago. Although the major stock exchanges have experienced substantial growth, the ECNs threaten to shift volumes for equity trade matching and clearance away from the traditional exchanges, in addition to applying tremendous price pressure. In fact, ECNs, once the exclusive domain of day traders and institutions, are raising money and partnering with online brokerage firms like E*TRADE to become mainstream trading mechanisms. In 1999 these systems already accounted for about 22 percent of Nasdaq trades. Some, such as Archipelago ECN, now have full-fledged stock exchange status. In response to the threats of new entrants, many traditional exchanges are upgrading their technologies, and even merging globally, in order to compete.

For example, the Amsterdam, Brussels, and Paris exchanges were merged in 2000 to form Euronext, the first pan-European exchange. As of December 2000, more than 1,600 companies were listed on Euronext, representing a market capitalization of EUR 2.420 billion. Average monthly trading volumes on the central electronic order book of EUR 142 billion (in 2000) instantly made Euronext one of the largest exchanges in Europe.

In July 2001 Euronext had its own initial public offering and stock market listing. In response, the Swiss Exchange (SWX) and the Tradepoint Consortium (which includes ECNs like Archipelago) set up a pan-European market for blue chip stocks called Virt-X for their first trade day in June 2001. Such mergers and alliances are forged to expand the user base of the companies involved, to achieve economies of scale, and to deter competitive entry.

Similarly, in the Dutch flower industry Flower Auction Holland and Flower Auction Flora merged in 2001 to form FloraHolland. The merger gave both auctions greater scale, as well as a larger operations and customer base to share the fixed costs of future investments in technology. The merger also gave suppliers and customers the opportunity for more efficient logistics given that the joint entity has four strategically located centers throughout Holland.

Mergers and acquisitions are also used as a global expansion strategy. eBay's global strategy, for instance, is built around merging with existing local online auctions in Europe and Asia. And indeed, eBay acquired iBazar in France and Internet Auction, the market leader in South Korea, to expand its presence, along with previously acquired or created sites in the United Kingdom, Germany, Austria, Canada, Japan, and Australia. eBay's acquisition and growth strategy has motivated competitors to follow suit. QXL and Ricardo—two of the largest European auctions—have merged, and a further shakeout of smaller local auction sites in European countries is underway. As traditional and electronic markets consolidate, we expect to see increased numbers of alliances, mergers, and acquisitions.

## *Leveraging Market Competencies*

Mergers and acquisitions can be used for growing or sustaining the value of existing markets. But market makers can also leverage their competence at market making to diversify. For example, Aucnet leveraged its core market-making expertise in Japan to diversify from used-car markets to those for motorcycles, flowers, and watches.

Indeed, leveraging market-making competencies into new industry sectors can be an extremely profitable strategy. This is especially true when new entrants can leverage new technologies to enter existing markets for standardized products. As ECNs have demonstrated, making markets in equities is relatively straightforward, given that equities are a well-defined and standardized product. That said, traditional market makers may want to look at leveraging their expertise into more complex financial instruments, from specialized fixed-income products to complex derivatives. Although these products may not have the volume of the equity market, they may provide greater margin and growth opportunities for market makers facing competition from ECNs.

## Rules for Market Ownership

A critical question for all market makers and participants is, Who should own the electronic markets? Should it be the buyer, the seller, or a third party? Should consortia or independent companies own the markets? Should companies set up their own private marketplaces? Furthermore, should these markets be for-profit or not-for-profit entities? Because the market owner carries the rights to profits generated as well as the costs of constructing and operating the market, these considerations are critical. The answer, of course, is a moving target, since the ownership may change over the life of the market.

Based on our analysis of numerous markets, we have come up with a simple rule: The market participants should choose the ownership structure that maximizes their operational benefits and profit potential from the market-making activity. That is, the owners of markets should generally be those who benefit the most from their operations.

But since markets often serve a large community of buyers and sellers, the costs of owning and operating a viable market may exceed the operational benefits and revenue potential that accrue to any one participant. In these cases, independent or consortia exchanges can be more viable. Consortia ownership allows the buyers and sellers to profit from the earnings of the market. Independent markets transfer both market costs and profits to a third party, be it private owners or public shareholders.

In figure 8-3, we summarize our ownership rule, in terms of the market benefits and costs to the participants in the markets.

The vertical axis of this figure defines the expected benefits as either proprietary or common. The horizontal axis categorizes the expected benefits as a proportion of the costs the participant would incur to make the specific market. The costs could include those related to getting suppliers or buyers to participate, the costs of getting the market to critical mass, and the costs of operating the exchange. Given its low expected benefits, quadrant 4 is especially unattractive.

In quadrant 1, a participant can expect little benefit, as either a seller or a buyer. The buyer or seller doesn't receive enough value to justify the costs of investment or ownership of the exchange. In this quadrant, then, an independent exchange is generally the best way to organize trades. This way, risks (and profits) are transferred to an independent third

**FIGURE 8-3**

## Models of Market Ownership

| Type of Benefit to Participants | Independent Exchanges | Consortia Exchanges |
|---|---|---|
| | **1** | **2** |
| Common | Provide a common platform to buyers and sellers—ideal for commodities with large numbers of buyers and/or sellers. | Provide a common platform to participants. Owned and driven by a subset of participants who wish to capture returns instead of sharing profits with third parties. |
| | **Not Attractive for Participants** | **Private Exchanges** |
| Proprietary | **4** | **3** |
| | | Provide a platform for trading that is proprietary to participants. Owner uses platform to maximize benefits for the firm. |

Low                                              High

**Level of Benefits as a Proportion of Costs Incurred to Make Market**

party who can aggregate a large number of trades among diverse participants and thus make a profit. This is the case among various independent exchanges.

In quadrant 2, participants can expect a high level of benefit relative to costs. These benefits, however, will be common to other buyers or sellers, and for that reason, will motivate the participants to form consortia exchanges, where they share the market ownership. In B2B electronic commerce, these consortia markets offer more than simple search, matching, and ordering capabilities. They increasingly serve as industry platforms for supply chain planning, collaboration, and order and logistics tracking. In quadrant 3, participants seek and receive great proprietary benefits relative to the costs of market creation and participation. In this case, private exchanges are a suitable model.

Changes in technology or industry structure can motivate changes in how markets are organized and owned. For example, the Dutch flower auctions were formed as cooperatives so that the growers could focus on growing their products, rather than selling them. The cooperative itself also benefited, accruing profits generated by transaction fees. The Tele Flower Auction was started due to the exclusion of East African and other imported flowers (which were depressing domestic flower prices at the time). In both the Dutch flower auctions and the Tele Flower Auction, the creation of the market was driven by the participants who would benefit most from them.

Like the flower auctions, many of the Dutch agricultural product markets were originally formed by supplier cooperatives. But now there is a trend toward even bigger buyers, such as large wholesalers and supermarket chains. Large buyers can bypass markets to select individual producers, even contracting to purchase in volume in the future. Alternatively, a consortium of larger buyers can form its own markets, employing trading methods that best suit the members.

As competition from these exchanges increases, other markets have moved to a more neutral model—going public and transferring ownership to the public. Some Dutch dairy product cooperatives, for example, have transferred ownership risk to the public sector, simultaneously raising capital to meet future competition. These markets, then, are dynamic, and change when profits diminish or external market changes warrant.

Ownership can also change in response to the need to increase scale, or the need to capitalize and provide greater customer convenience. Nasdaq, the second largest stock exchange in the world (based on market capitalization of listed companies), for instance, is owned and operated by the National Association of Securities Dealers (NASD), a non-profit organization of broker-dealers originally set up to self-regulate the industry. Today Nasdaq is faced with challenges ranging from globalization and price pressure to new competitors like ECNs. In response, the NASD has taken the first steps to spinning out Nasdaq as a public company—having first issued a private placement of shares in Nasdaq to its members. Going public will provide capital for investment and expansion and transfer ownership and ownership risks to the public shareholders.

## Building Market Strategies

Making markets in various industry verticals is not the core business of most firms. Instead, most businesses build a product or offer a service to meet customer needs better than a competitor. For these companies, markets and auctions are a tool to gain new efficiencies in the supply chain, provide better coordination, gain information leverage with buyers and suppliers, or manage inventory through resale. For other firms, emerging market applications will be used to improve resource allocation and decision making within the firm. As a manager, you will have to decide how to select and use markets as a tool to support your strategic objectives.

We believe there are three key steps to building an electronic market strategy.

### Creating an Electronic Markets Vision

The first step toward using electronic markets effectively is to envision where it can create value for your firm. Will the creation of a buy-side consortium electronic market create the most value for your business? Or will a private exchange to your key customers (like the Cisco Connection) create the greatest value?

By building on the applications described in this book— from procurement auctions to markets for prediction and decision making—managers can identify potential market applications and opportunities for new value creation. The process/stakeholder benefit framework in chapter 3 can also be used to systematically assess the likely value and cost of each opportunity. These tools can help prioritize initiatives and guide the selection and implementation of the firm's electronic market portfolio.

## Selecting Strategies for Market Implementation and Participation

There are many ways in which companies can participate in markets. As we discussed in chapter 5, companies can choose to buy market access from an independent third-party market maker, participate in or even co-own a consortium marketplace, or build their own private market application.

If your company will be participating in electronic markets owned by others, you must decide which markets are aligned with your business strategy and how to effectively integrate your company into those markets. The rule for participation is increasingly "follow the liquidity" to where the greatest value can be found. The greater the liquidity and participation of buyers and sellers, the easier it will be to buy and sell products and create value. Consider the Dell auctions for used computers. This was a good idea initially, but as eBay becomes the dominant computer resale platform with the greatest liquidity (over 42 million users), Dell is having an increasingly difficult time maintaining a separate auction market for itself. This has motivated IBM and Sun Microsystems to use eBay to clear their merchandise.

Next, one needs to develop an integration strategy with the third-party market. As we saw in chapter 5, connecting to B2B markets is challenging, requiring considerable technical and organizational investments to realize value.

If you are going to build a private exchange or establish an independent or consortium electronic market, you will have to decide how to do this cost effectively. Fortunately, new software tools and third-party service providers make the creation of markets easier. You can even hire third parties to host market-making services online, customizing them to your market needs. As we discussed in chapter 3, various companies now serve as application service providers, offering specific market-making services such as online auction capabilities.

How to assemble all the services required to make a marketplace involves many considerations. For example, will markets constructed through hosted services scale well to the needs of different buyers and sellers? Will the hosted marketplace be secure enough for the needs of buyers and sellers? Will you have enough control to modify the structure of the marketplace to meet the evolving needs of buyers and sellers? Fortunately, many of these concerns can now be addressed well by third parties. In fact, we anticipate that more electronic market initiatives will be outsourced to third parties for hosting. This will apply to markets in the supply chain as well as to internal markets.

For security and privacy reasons, internal markets for prediction and decision making may seem like ideal candidates for the firm to build and host on its own servers. But this may not always be the case. Consider a market designed to surface managers' beliefs about, and assign values to, various corporate initiatives. This market could be structured so that different knowledgeable managers could buy and trade stock in different initiatives. The price a manager is willing to pay for stock in an initiative expresses his or her belief in the value of the initiative. Managers may also express opinions on the future value of the stock (initiative) on a message board. Participants may want to keep their investments in different initiatives private and communicate aggregate price information only to the executive sponsors of the market. The participants may also want to anonymously express their beliefs about different stocks so that they are not penalized. In this case, a third-party service provider can play a critical role in maintaining this anonymity.

Whatever strategy you undertake to deploy an electronic market—build, assemble from off-the-shelf components and services, or rent—we have found that successful market makers and participants invest in detailed implementation plans, ones that determine how resources will be directed to bridge the gap between existing systems, processes, and capabilities and those required for the envisioned electronic markets. These plans must also address application requirements, vendor evaluations, and the assessment of alternative market configurations. They should also determine how participants in the new market, inside and outside the firm, should be mobilized to make it a reality.

### Mobilizing for Market Implementation

To build and implement an electronic market, companies must assemble the key capabilities for executing their vision. For B2B markets, these include the technical expertise either to assemble the marketplace components or to integrate the electronic market software and data with the firm's legacy systems and supply chain. Different types of technical expertise will be required for other types of market applications.

Beyond technical expertise, the greater challenge will be mobilizing the organization or its key trading partners to participate in the market. This will require some retraining of staff as well as changes in job roles, work flow, and processes. Mobilizing suppliers and buyers, meanwhile, may involve minimal training, but may require broader investments such as software and consulting services to enable suppliers to participate. As we noted in chapter 3, new markets disrupt the status quo and the existing relationships between traders and market makers. To encourage the transition, a new market should help participants overcome the cost and the challenges so that they can effectively integrate into the new marketplace. In this way the market will create compelling value for all.

Sometimes the expertise and capabilities required to mobilize the organization are available in-house. Other times, they will have to be outsourced. Large companies participating in multiple markets are likely to have the scale to justify dedicated, specialized resources to create and maintain the new electronic markets. As discussed in chapter 5, the Dow Chemical Company illustrates one way of doing this.

Beyond the technical and organizational resources, leadership is another critical ingredient. At General Electric, it was the senior executive support that legitimized and encouraged the adoption of new market initiatives inside and outside the firm. It was important for these leaders to encourage experimentation and "learning by doing." As there is no single best way to design and implement markets, those organizations that engage in multiple market initiatives will gain the most experience and seize the value of markets most quickly.

## Keeping an Eye on the Future

Smart managers not only develop and execute dynamic strategies for the present, but also do so with an eye on future developments. From today's all-in-one markets to multi-attribute and combinatorial auctions, technology continues to enable new ways of trading that meet the varied risk, information, transaction cost, and trade volume preferences of participants.

In the future we can expect far more computationally complex and advanced methods of trading that leverage increased computing power. Novel combinatorial auction methods will be applied to maximize the utility of multiple traders seeking to trade different baskets of goods. Such a computationally intensive application in equities markets could permit mutual funds to rebalance their portfolios at low transaction costs. For instance, these new auctions would allow each mutual fund to put up a whole basket of equities to purchase or sell. The computer algorithms would reassign parts of each basket to new owners in such a manner that all participants realize the maximum possible benefit.

In addition to new market mechanisms, new types of software agents or "bots" will evolve to support participation in markets and help conserve the buyer's attention—the scarcest resource in today's economy. These tools may traverse markets and networks, for instance, to search for items on the buyer's behalf, and then, like program trading, negotiate and buy it for him. In some markets, these programs may someday perform better than humans. They may not be subject to the anchoring and adjustment biases or the other bidding problems discussed in chapter 7.

As we have stated throughout this book, we believe that electronic markets will continue to grow and have diverse and strategic business applications. Many of these applications are still in their infancy, but we predict that in the course of this decade, they will become part of common business practices.

Specifically, we can expect the greater use of market mechanisms within and across firms for decision making and knowledge management. As we move to a knowledge economy, the best ideas and know-how do not reside in a central repository, but are dispersed in the minds of staffers and experts worldwide. To compete effectively, executives must be able to find and extract that relevant knowledge. The next generations of prediction and knowledge markets will provide incentives to workers and experts to share knowledge, reveal beliefs, and improve decision-making and resource allocation processes. The power of auctions to socially construct value can also be applied to the vexing problem of valuing the intangible assets of the firm. Implementing these market mechanisms for decision making and the assignation of value within firms will require enlightened leadership and executive commitment. After all, markets will be more than a little threatening to some managers used to hierarchical models of decision making and resource allocation. Yet as companies realize the value of markets, they will adapt to this innovation by balancing the individuals' needs for safety and certainty found in hierarchies with the resource mobility, value creation opportunities, and freedom of choice enabled by markets.

As computing becomes more ubiquitous, new technologies, like radio frequency identity tags, will be dispersed through the value chain. Market mechanisms will then be used for machine-to-machine or "silent" commerce. Parts or perishables, for instance, may "signal" their availability for production. Using market algorithms, only those products that would bring the highest value to the firm at the time would be assembled.

Many of the above innovations will initially outrun the capacity of users to absorb them. But over time, we expect users will create a new social consensus on how to make them work. As we venture to new market spaces, we have a long way to go to learning how best to design and implement these markets.

In the past, our access to information and our ability to process it was difficult. Today information is increasingly abundant, but our attention is scarce. Our previous models of markets and organizations predicated on information scarcity and transaction cost economics will now have to be revised to account for attention scarcity. Furthermore, we know little about human behavior in markets. Consider the winner's curse, or how individuals respond to negative versus positive ratings, or their responses to different ways of representing products. Our models and theories of human market behavior are still in their infancy. While we hope this book will stimulate managers toward the greater use of markets, we also hope it will stimulate practitioners and researchers to collaborate and learn how to design markets from a pragmatic and broader interdisciplinary perspective. As you can see, electronic markets have a great future. Or better said, the future is almost limitless.

# Epilogue

## A Call to Action

IN WRITING THIS BOOK we wanted to share our enthusiasm for electronic markets and the opportunities to use them in new ways to create business value. We hope you now find markets more exciting and much richer than the textbook abstraction typically conveyed in an economics class.

A couple of weeks ago I was invited to give a lecture on auctions in a marketing class taught by Professor Bruce Weinberg of Bentley College. Bruce is a gifted teacher and he had asked all his students to sell something on eBay, Yahoo!, or another auction before coming to class. As I heard descriptions of students selling a used pair of Nike sneakers for $51 to a buyer in Germany, a CD changer, or a one-of-kind lamp, I realized what even the best book could not do. Ultimately, to really understand the profound transformation of markets, you have to experience and engage them.

As busy executives you may not have made the time to trade in an auction other than the stock market. To really master the new opportunities it is imperative to engage, so we invite you—go up to your attic and put something up for sale. More than 42 million people already have done so on eBay, as have millions of others on Yahoo! and other sites.

We also invite you to http://www.makingmarkets.com, a
Web site we have created to point to useful resources on auctions and exchanges.

May you bid profitably!

*Ajit Kambil and Eric van Heck*

# Notes

## Chapter 1

1. 1999 revenues are from PartMiner's S1 statement filed February 18, 2000; 2000 revenues are from Deloitte & Touche's Technology Fast 500 list for 2001. See <http://www.public. deloitte.com/fast500/>.

2. Accessible through <http://www.tfa.nl>.

3. See Miguel Helft, "What Makes eBay Unstoppable?" *Industry Standard*, 6 August 2001.

4. Accessible through <http://www.chemconnect.com>.

5. Dow Chemical, "Dow Chooses ChemConnect as Their Preferred Internet Exchange," *Corporate News*, 22 November 1999.

6. See Ronald H. Coase's classic paper, "The Nature of the Firm," *Economica* 4 (1937): 386–405.

7. See O. E. Williamson's book, *Markets and Hierarchies, Analysis and Anti-Trust Implications: A Study on the Economics of Internal Organization* (New York: Free Press, 1975). For further development of these concepts, see O. E. Williamson, *The Economic Institutions of Capitalism: Firms, Markets, Relational Contracting* (New York: Free Press, 1985).

8. This proposition was first developed by Tom W. Malone, Joanne Yates, and Robert I. Benjamin in their classic article, "Electronic Markets and Electronic Hierarchies," *Communications of the ACM* 30, no. 6 (July 1987): 484–497.

## Chapter 2

1. New York Stock Exchange, *The New York Stock Exchange 1792–1992: The First 200 Years* (New York: Greenwich Publishing Group, 1992).

203

2. These market processes are adapted from their first classification as critical exchange-related tasks in Ajit Kambil, "Electronic Integration: Designing Information Technology Mediated Exchange Relations and Networks" (Ph.D. diss., MIT Sloan School of Management, 1993). The diagram is adapted from Ajit Kambil, "Doing Business in the Wired World," *IEEE Computer,* May 1997, 58.

3. For an analysis of how companies can effectively use dynamic pricing, see Ajit Kambil and Vipul Agrawal, "The New Realities of Dynamic Pricing," *Outlook* 13, no. 2 (July 2001): 14–21. *Outlook* is published by Accenture.

4. George Akerlof, "The Market for Lemons: Qualitative Uncertainty and the Market Mechanism," *Quarterly Journal of Economics* 84 (1970): 488–500.

5. For more, see K. J. Arrow, *The Limits of Organization* (New York: Norton, 1974), 23.

6. Accessible through <http://www.aerome.com>.

7. Accessible through <http://www.rosettanet.org>.

8. More information on XML can found at <http://computer.org/internet/xml/> and <http://www.w3.org/XML/>.

9. See Andre Bergholz, "Extending Your Markup: An XML Tutorial," *IEEE Internet Computing,* July/August 2000, 74–79.

## Chapter 3

1. Accessible through <http://www.harborsideplus.com>.

2. For more information on FloraHolland, see <http://www.floraholland.nl>.

3. For more information on the Aalsmeer Flower Auction, see <http://www.vba.com>.

4. From Joshua D. Coval and Tyler Shumway, "Is Sound Just Noise?" working paper, University of Michigan Business School, Ann Arbor, January 2000.

5. Exmtrade is a fictitious name for a real company.

6. Accessible through <http://www.aucnet.co.jp>.

7. See David Allen, "New Telecommunications Services: Network Externalities and Critical Mass," *Telecommunications Policy,* September 1988, 257–271.

8. The process/stakeholder benefit framework for the Dutch flower markets was originally published in Ajit Kambil and Eric van Heck, "Re-engineering the Dutch Flower Auctions: A Framework for Analyzing Exchange Organizations," *Information Systems Research 9,* no. 1 (March 1998): 1–19.

9. See Jochem A. Paarlberg, "Web Auctions in Europe: An Analysis of 194 Consumer Web Auctions in Eight European Countries" (M.Sc. thesis, Rotterdam School of Management, Rotterdam, June 2001).

## Chapter 4

1. In Michael Schrage, "To Hal Varian, the Price Is Always Right," *Business & Strategy* 18 (2000): 82–93.

2. Accessible through <http://www.tiredex.com/cgi-bin/tdexin-dex.pl>.

3. For more details, see David Lucking-Reiley, "Vickrey Auctions in Practice: From Nineteenth Century Philately to Twenty-first Century E-commerce," *Journal of Economic Perspectives* 14, no. 3 (2000): 183–192.

4. See Martin Bichler, "An Experimental Analysis of Multi-attribute Auctions," *Decision Support Systems* 29, no. 3 (October 2000): 249–268.

5. See Otto Koppius and Eric van Heck, "Information Architecture and Electronic Market Performance: The Case of Multi-dimensional Auctions" (paper presented at the INFORMS Annual Meeting, Miami Beach, November 2001).

6. For a detailed discussion of combinatorial auctions, see M. H. Rothkopf, A. Pekec, and R. M. Harstad, "Computationally Manageable Combinatorial Auctions," *Management Science* 44, no. 8 (1998): 1131–1147.

7. Accessible through <http://www.homedepot.com>.

8. We owe the Home Depot example to Pinar Keskinocak and Sridhar Tayur, "Quantitative Analysis for Internet-Enabled Supply Chains," *Interfaces* 30, no. 2 (March/April 2001): 70–89. See <http://www.informs.org/ebiz/interfaces/>.

9. For more information, see the discussion of additional bidders in J. I. Bulow and P. D. Klemperer, "Auctions vs. Negotiations," *American Economic Review* 86 (1996): 180–194.

10. They call them Dutch auctions, which strictly speaking is not true—a Dutch auction is a descending, not ascending, price auction.

11. For a summary of this study, see Steve Lohr, "Compressed Data; Professors Study Method for Doing Well on eBay," *New York Times*, 26 November 2001.

12. Otto Koppius, Eric van Heck, and Matthijs Wolters, "Product Representation and Price Formation in Screen Auctions:

Empirical Results from a Dutch Flower Auction," *Proceedings of the First International Conference on Telecommunications and Electronic Commerce (ICTEC)*, eds. Bezalel Gavish and Amit Basu (Nashville, TN: Vanderbilt University, 1998): 178–186.

13. Otto Koppius, Virpi Tuunainen, and Eric van Heck, "Auction Speed as a Design Variable for Internet Auctions" (paper presented at the INFORMS Annual Meeting, Miami Beach, November 2001).

14. David Lucking-Reiley, Doug Bryan, Naghi Prasad, and Daniel Reeves, "Pennies from eBay: the Determinants of Price in Online Auctions," working paper, Accenture Technology Labs, Chicago, November 1999.

15. Gerald Hauble and Peter Popowski Leszczyc, "Going, Going, Gone—Determinants of Bidding Behavior and Selling Prices in Internet Auctions" (paper presented at the Second INFORMS Conference on Internet Marketing, University of Southern California, Los Angeles, August 2000).

16. See Paul L. Joskow, "California's Electricity Crisis," working paper, MIT Center for Energy and Environmental Policy Research, Cambridge, July 2001.

17. Ibid.

## Chapter 5

1. This chapter builds on the following Accenture studies, points of view, and reports: Jeff Brooks and Roger W. Dik, "B2B eMarkets: The Smart Path Forward," *Supply Chain Perspectives*, Summer 2001. *Supply Chain Perspectives* is published by Accenture. C. Edwin Starr, Ajit Kambil, Jonathan D. Whitaker, and Jeffrey D. Brooks, "One Size Does Not Fit All—The Need for an E-Marketplace Portfolio," *ASCET* 3 (1 May 2001): 96–99; Ajit Kambil and Donald Chartier, "Don't Fail at B2B, Manage the Organizational and Human Factors," research note, Accenture Institute for Strategic Change, 13 July 2001; Ajit Kambil and M. Scott Sparks, "Seizing the Value of e-Procurement Auctions," *Supply Chain eBusiness* 2, no. 1 (February 2001): 53–54; and William C. Copacino and Roger W. Dik, "Why B2B eMarkets Are Here to Stay," *Outlook* 13, no. 2 (July 2001): 22–29. *Outlook* is published by Accenture.

2. Based on work with many clients by the Accenture Dynamic Pricing Solutions Service.

3. Jupiter Research, "Industry-Sponsored Marketplaces," October 2000.

4. For more information, see William C. Copacino and Roger W. Dik, "Why B2B eMarkets Are Here to Stay," *Outlook* 13, no. 2 (July 2001): 22–29. *Outlook* is published by Accenture.

5. Ibid.

6. Thomas H. Davenport, Jeffrey D. Brooks, and Susan Cantrell, The Dynamics of eCommerce Networks. Accenture Institute for Strategic Change Working Paper, 1 February 2001.

## Chapter 6

1. See <http://www.gcrio.org/OnLnDoc/pdf/pdf/morgheim000 921.pdf> for a copy of the statement by Jeff Morgheim, BP Climate Change Manager, to the Senate Committee on Commerce, Science, and Transportation hearing on solutions to reduce greenhouse gas emissions, 21 September 2000. For a status report on the program as of May 2001, see <http://www.bpamoco.com/downloads/340/ghg_ emissions_trading_in_bp_may2001.pdf>.

2. This section on resale markets is adapted from Paul Nunes and Julia Kirby, "What Goes Around Comes Around," *Outlook* 12, no. 1 (2000): 37–41. *Outlook* is an Accenture publication. Adapted with permission.

3. Accessible through <http://www.dellauction.com>.

4. For a detailed analysis, see Moritz Fleischmann, "Quantitative Models for Reverse Logistics" (Ph.D. diss., Rotterdam School of Management, Erasmus University, 2000).

5. See Julie Dunn, "Five Questions for Michele Burns; How an Airline Burns Less Money," *New York Times*, 22 October 2000.

6. Ibid.

7. See Peter L. Bernstein, *Against the Gods—The Remarkable Story of Risk* (New York: John Wiley & Sons, 1996), 305.

8. Dunn, "Five Questions for Michele Burns."

9. Pankaj Ghemawat and David Lane, "Enron: Entrepreneurial Energy," Case N9-700-079 (Boston: Harvard Business School, 2000).

10. Accessible through <http://www.enron.com>.

11. See Robert Westervelt, "Futures Come Into Focus," *Chemical Week*, 15 August 2001. CheMatch was acquired by ChemConnect in January 2001.

12. Bernstein, *Against the Gods*.

13. See also Darnell Little, "This Future Exchange Isn't About Soybeans," *Business Week*, 9 October 2000.

14. See Hal R. Varian, "Effect of the Internet on Financial Markets," working paper, University of California, Berkeley, September 1998.

15. Accessible through <http://www.biz.uiowa.edu/iem/>.

16. See Charles Plott, "Markets as Information Gathering Tools," *Southern Economic Journal* 67, no. 1 (July 2000): 2–12.

17. We owe this example to Anita Chabria, "Can This Virtual Market Tell Tinseltown What'll Sell?" *Business Week Online*, 3 November 2000.

18. See David M. Pennock and Steve Lawrence, "Extracting Collective Probabilistic Forecasts from Web Games," *Proceedings of the Seventh ACM SIGKDD International Conference on Knowledge Discovery and Data Mining* (New York: ACM, 2001).

19. See David M. Pennock, Steve Lawrence, C. Lee Giles, and Finn Arup Nielsen, "The Real Power of Artificial Markets," *Science* 291 (9 February 2001): 987–988 (Letters).

## Chapter 7

1. See Ajit Kambil and Vipul Agrawal, "The New Realities of Dynamic Pricing," *Outlook* 13, no. 2 (July 2001): 19. *Outlook* is published by Accenture.

2. See Youngme Moon, "Onsale, Inc.," Case 9-599-091 (Boston: Harvard Business School Publishing, May 1999). Onsale.com is now a part of Egghead.com. Egghead's assets were bought by Amazon.com in December 2001.

3. See C. Avery, "Strategic Jump Bidding in English Auctions," *The Review of Economic Studies* 65, no. 2 (1998): 185–210; and Michel Fishman, "A Theory of Preemptive Takeover Bidding," *Rand Journal of Economics* 19, no. 1 (Spring 1988): 88–101.

4. For other bidding strategies, see "Bargaining and Auctions," in Douglas D. Davis and Charles A. Holt, *Experimental Economics* (Princeton, NJ: Princeton University Press, 1993), 241–316.

5. For sealed-bid first-price auctions with $N$ bidders and private value $v_i$ for the $i^{th}$ bidder, the optimal strategy is to bid the value $b$:

$b_i = (1 - 1/N)\ [v_i]$, where $b_i$ is the bid by the $i^{th}$ bidder, for $i = 1\ ...N$.

Naturally, as $N$ gets large, this approximates the true value to the bidder $[v_i]$.

6. We owe this example to Michael Schrage, "To Hal Varian, the Price Is Always Right," *Business & Strategy* 18 (2000): 82–93. The

auction tournament is described in more detail in John Rust and Daniel Friedman, *The Double Auction Market: Institutions, Theories, and Evidence* (Reading, MA: Addison-Wesley, 1993).

7. There are four sources for discussions and summaries of evidence: Douglas D. Davis and Charles A. Holt, *Experimental Economics* (Princeton, NJ: Princeton University Press, 1993); J. H. Kagel and A. E. Roth, eds., *The Handbook of Experimental Economics* (Princeton, NJ: Princeton University Press, 1995); Richard H. Thaler, "The Winner's Curse," *Across the Board,* September 1992, 30–33; and Douglas Dyer and John H. Kagel, "Bidding in Common Value Auctions: How the Commercial Construction Industry Corrects for the Winner's Curse," *Management Science* 42, no. 10 (October 1996): 1463–1475.

8. See Thomas Kern, Leslie Willcocks, and Eric van Heck, "The Winner's Curse in IT Outsourcing: Strategies for Avoiding Relational Trauma," *California Management Review* 44, no. 2 (2002): 47–69.

9. For a fuller discussion, see Charles A. Holt and Roger Sherman, "The Loser's Curse," *American Economic Review* 84, no. 3 (June 1994): 642–652.

10. A classic demonstration for this effect is found in I. Simonson and A. Tversky, "Choice in Context: Tradeoff Contrast and Extremeness Aversion," *Journal of Marketing Research* 29 (1992): 281–295.

11. See Joseph C. Nunes and Peter Boatwright, "Price Encounters," *Harvard Business Review*, July–August 2001, 18–19.

## Chapter 8

1. For more on all-in-one markets, see Ajit Kambil, Paul F. Nunes, and Diane Wilson, "Transforming the Marketspace with All-in-One Markets," *International Journal of Electronic Commerce* 3, no. 4 (1999): 11–28; or Paul Nunes, Diane Wilson, and Ajit Kambil, "The All-in-One Market," *Harvard Business Review*, May–June 2000, 19–20.

# Index

# About the Authors

AJIT KAMBIL is an Associate Partner and Senior Research Fellow at the Accenture Institute for Strategic Change, where he leads electronic commerce, supply chain, and innovation research initiatives. He is also an Executive Researcher in Residence at Babson College. Kambil has studied the effective design and deployment of markets for more than a decade. In his work at Accenture on fast venturing, he has devised new ways for companies to bring innovations to markets through partnerships, and in his work on co-creation and value innovation, he has identified strategies for creating new products and markets that leverage the power of the Internet. Prior to joining Accenture, Kambil was on the faculty of New York University's Stern School of Business, where he introduced electronic commerce into the M.B.A. program and led the National Science Foundation–funded project to put the Securities and Exchange Commission's EDGAR database on the Internet, empowering investors worldwide with free access to corporate disclosure documents.

Kambil is a frequent industry speaker and is widely published in a number of business and technical journals, including the *Harvard Business Review, Sloan Management Review, Communications of the ACM, Management Science,* and *IEEE Computer.* He serves on the editorial board of the *International Journal of Electronic Markets* and the *International Journal of Electronic Commerce.* He holds an S.M. in Technology and Policy and an S.M. and Ph.D. in Management Science with a concentration in Information Technologies from MIT. Kambil can be reached at akambil@ alum.mit.edu.

ERIC VAN HECK is a Professor of Business Administration at Erasmus University's Rotterdam School of Management, where he teaches in the international M.B.A. program and in the Global eManagement (GeM) program. His research concentrates on the design of electronic markets and on the design of business modularization. In his research he helps companies to develop innovative electronic auctions. He is a member of the Erasmus Research Institute of Management. Prior to joining Erasmus University, van Heck was a Research Fellow at Tilburg University, an Assistant Professor at Wageningen University, and a visiting scholar at New York University, and he has worked for Cap Gemini.

Van Heck has published in journals such as the *California Management Review, Communications of the ACM, Harvard Business Review, Information Systems Research,* and *Wirtschafts-Informatik.* He is a member of the editorial board of *Electronic Commerce Research* and the *Journal of Information Technology* and has written or edited twelve books. Van Heck received both his M.Sc. and Ph.D. from Wageningen University. His home page is http://people.fbk.eur.nl/eheck/.